MISS
WORLD
1970

MISS WORLD 1970

HOW I ENTERED A PAGEANT AND WOUND UP MAKING HISTORY

JENNIFER HOSTEN

sh.
SUTHERLAND
HOUSE

TORONTO, 2020

Sutherland House
416 Moore Ave., Suite 205
Toronto, ON M4G 1C9

First edition, February 2020

If you are interested in inviting one of our authors to a live event or media appearance, please contact publicity@sutherlandhousebooks.com and visit our website at sutherlandhousebooks.com for more information about our authors and their schedules.

Manufactured in the United States
Cover designed by Lena Yang
Book composed by Karl Hunt
Cover photo courtesy of Getty Images

Library and Archives Canada Cataloguing in Publication
Title: Miss World 1970 : How I entered a pageant and
wound up making history / Jennifer Hosten ;
Names: Hosten-Craig, Jennifer, author.
Identifiers: Canadiana 20200154230 | ISBN 9781989555231 (hardcover)
Subjects: LCSH: Hosten-Craig, Jennifer. | LCSH: Beauty contestants—
Grenada—Biography. | LCSH: Beauty contests—History—20th century. |
LCSH: Miss World Pageant. | LCSH: Diplomats—Grenada—Biography.
Classification: LCC HQ1220.G84 H67 2020 |
DDC 791.6/6092—dc23

ISBN 978-1-9895552-3-1

FOREWORD

I FIRST MET JENNIFER HOSTEN for breakfast in Grenada. I somehow knew it was her from her poised posture and the calm, regal energy she exuded as I approached the open-air restaurant overlooking the island's famously endless Grand Anse beach.

I have to admit, I was a little nervous to meet finally this Miss World pioneer, who in 1970 was the first woman of colour to win the title in one of the most intersectional and controversial contests in the competition's history, hijacked by the newly formed women's liberation movement on live television and watched by millions. The contest arguably became a springboard for 1970s feminism.

I was about to play Jennifer in a major movie based on those events. I was researching the role at the height of 2018's #MeToo and Time's Up movements, having been on my first women's march one year earlier. With conversations about representation, gender, misogyny and abuse of power reverberating in the zeitgeist from Hollywood to every industry, corporation, and beyond, it felt like the perfect time to learn from someone who inadvertently became the poster child for these issues in a very different era.

I had so much to ask her but I also wanted to observe her essence and breathe her in, in the context of the island of which she *was* and, as I would discover, will *always* be queen.

We'd spoken briefly on the phone and exchanged a couple of emails in which I'd boldly suggested meeting in Grenada to fulfil my romantic research fantasy. To my disappointment, the whole film was to be shot in the United Kingdom—the pageant had taken place in London—so no exotic James Bond-style shoots on this Caribbean spice island, no flashbacks to Jennifer winning Miss Grenada on the beach, just London in December and my imagination, which I was determined to fuel on this trip!

I was delighted that Jennifer agreed to join me in Grenada, but in that moment, approaching our breakfast, butterflies arose within me. Jennifer, now based in Canada, and myself, having travelled from London, had both taken a leap of faith in deciding to meet. Jennifer was accompanied by her daughter Sophia. I had brought my Mum along for a break from the British winter. Couldn't it all be terribly awkward? Couldn't it all go horribly wrong?

Once I drew closer, those unmistakable deep brown eyes locked me in. Bright and burning with intelligence and wisdom, they looked into my soul and stilled my apprehension.

Reading the script for our film, *Misbehaviour,* was my first intro-duction to the historic events of Miss World 1970. Growing up, as I did, in 1980s and 1990s Oxfordshire, Miss World was not some-thing of which I was aware. I'd never seen it on TV and certainly had no contact with the world of pageants in my childhood or teens. I was never considered "a beauty" and although I loved dance and drama, it was never competitive. I suppose, as someone brought up and praised for what was inside my mind as opposed to how I looked, I, like many of my generation and culture, viewed beauty pageants with a mild disdain, dismissing them as an arena of the vacuous and superficial.

Talking with Jennifer, wise and well-travelled and now a trained psychotherapist, opened my mind. The thing that struck me most was that, at the time, she saw the competition as an opportunity and a stepping stone to a bigger life. What I learned to appreciate is that in that period Grenada still did not have its independence from Britain and 1970, the first year that Grenada had entered the competition, was a chance to put her small island on the map.

Jennifer took her role seriously as an ambassador for her country. The potential for the contest to open doors for her in the realm of broadcasting was a strong motivation and without taking it too seriously, she saw it as a means to an end and an enriching experience.

As her sister Pommie always said, winning a pageant requires "a package deal." Jennifer knew that physical beauty was just one facet of what made someone attractive, and that intelligence, grace and personality would also need to be paramount if she were to gain an edge.

Watching the recording of the actual pageant was still a strangely uncomfortable experience for me. The misogynistic tone and language used by Bob Hope and the tight smiles of the contestants as they were objectified beyond belief—asked to turn their behinds to the crowd for better inspection—made me sputter in offense. Jennifer's daughter Sophia shared my outrage. It was a moment that Philippa Lowthorpe, the director of "Misbehaviour," was keen to highlight, but at least in our film the moment is firmly rooted in the female gaze.

I also appreciated the nuances of Miss South Africa and Miss Africa South in the script, with South Africa shamed into submitting a black contestant for the first time, at the last minute, alongside its white contestant. It sounds absurd today for one nation to submit two women of different complexions, but with the anti-Apartheid campaign at its height, beauty had become politicised to powerful effect.

I was keen to capture Jennifer's pragmatic and centred intelligence in my portrayal of her, and over the four special days that we spent together in Grenada, I had time to discover more details that would help me honour her spirit in the role. I ran barefoot in the sand the length of Grand Anse beach as she had done to get in shape

shape for the contest. We explored the town of St. George's where as a girl she'd seen Joan Collins and Harry Belafonte film *Island In the Sun*. We walked the street where she grew up and visited the house where she spent her summer holidays. All the while, I listened to the music of her unique accent. Jennifer was kind enough to record her mother's poem, "Ode To Grenada," into my iPhone with the waves lapping in the background and I listened to it in my trailer most days on set.

Jennifer even offered to lend me for the film the original gold evening gown that she wore in the competition. Perfectly preserved, the striking gold crochet gown arrived in a shoebox shortly after our Grenada trip. Although the scene in which I wear it in the film is brief, it was very special and evocative for me to be able to wear the original dress for that moment and also for the photoshoot for the *Misbehaviour* film poster (which is the cover of the book you are holding).

Her celebrity status still casts its spell in her homeland. Everywhere we went, someone would approach "Miss Jennifer" for a chat and a catch-up and Jennifer would oblige with warm sincerity. In one especially moving moment as we were leaving a local waterfall, we met an elderly lady selling tourist souvenirs. She was shocked to see Jennifer. She remembered attending the original Miss Grenada competition, and watching Jennifer as a girl. The memories brought tears to her eyes. She grabbed Jennifer by both hands in disbelief. It touched me deeply and I began to understand what an iconic inspiration she has been and how much pride still glows for what she represents to so many people. It made me think of her legacy.

As I write this at the dawn of 2020, for the first time in history, Miss World, Miss Universe, Miss USA, Miss Teen USA, and Miss America are all women of colour. What does this mean? One could argue that there is still progress to be made in terms of how women are objectified in our culture. Yet there is also so much power in being represented, in feeling seen, and in having choices in life. It matters who gets to be celebrated. Cultural beauty standards and the optics of who we value as a winner give a message of belonging and self-esteem at a deep, subliminal level.

Before Beyoncé, before Rhianna, before Zendaya, there was Jennifer Hosten, a true trailblazer, an icon to inspire the next generation to know that they are seen and valued on the world stage.

This is her story.

Gugu Mbatha-Raw
Los Angeles, 2020

CONTENTS

The Big Stage

EARLY ON THE EVENING of the pageant, my sister Pommie and I walked out of the Britannia Hotel in London and climbed onto one of the long buses provided for Miss World 1970 contestants. We were by now familiar with the buses, and quite at home in them. They had been moving us back and forth to rehearsals and other events in the days leading up to the main event. When we found our seats, Pommie said to me, "Jen, do you like the way the hairdresser has done your hair? I think it could have been higher."

"Oh yes," I answered. "I like it. The crown, you see, will fit nicely just here."

Pommie laughed and said that she was happy to see me so confident.

I cannot explain the confidence that possessed me on the evening of November 20, 1970, but I was definitely feeling it. Pommie had helped. She was much more than my older sister. She was my friend and confidant, and my guide to the world of style and fashion. To my mind, she was the most attractive and charismatic member of our family. Earlier that evening, she had appeared at my door to help me dress, wearing a smashing low-cut black evening dress, and announced: "Jen, I am wearing black in mourning for the other girls tonight." Her confidence gave me confidence.

I did feel good about my hair, and my makeup and my jewellery too. And in the garment bags that Pommie and I lugged onto the coach, amid my stockings, my bathing suit and other items, was my secret weapon, my gorgeous gold evening gown. It was unique, a stunning creation (it would still stand out today). I knew it was spectacular, and I had carefully kept it under wraps, wearing another gown to the dress rehearsal. I did not want to reveal it until just the right moment.

But perhaps the biggest reason that I felt confident was that I was well prepared. Twenty-four hours earlier, that had not been the case. We had been at the Royal Albert Hall for what was supposed to be a complete dress rehearsal. All fifty-eight contestants, our chaperones, members of the press and the pageant organizers were supposed to run through the entire proceedings, just as we would the night after. As we were getting under way, Eric Morley, the head of Mecca, organizer of the Miss World pageant, took the stage, opened a piece of paper and called the names of fifteen girls. The chosen fifteen, he said, would go through the routine from start to finish. He gave the other forty-three girls permission to sit in the audience and observe the proceedings.

Needless to say, his announcement demoralized the forty-three contestants who looked on. Fifteen was the number of contestants who would survive the first elimination in the pageant. I was on the outside, one of the forty-three. We all felt that Morley had already made his choice of these fifteen finalists and the rest of us were surplus. We need not even rehearse (we had been on the stage before but not in our gowns and full heels, which is an entirely different proposition). It seemed only fair that we should be able to take a practice walk across the hall's enormous and somewhat complicated stage. We were crushed.

I don't think we were overreacting in the moment. It seemed to the press, as well, that the girls up onstage were the chosen few, and there would be captions in the papers the following morning highlighting the lucky fifteen. The contestants given the advantage of the full rehearsal also thought Morley's actions were significant. Miss Sweden, Miss Australia and Miss Norway—all but one of the fifteen were white, and a non-white girl had never won the Miss World contest—began to act in a most condescending manner to those who were not chosen.

Pommie sat with me in the audience, watching the rehearsal. She tried to lift my spirits by saying that it was very bad luck for a girl to try on the crown prior to the big event. I recalled that nearly all the select fifteen had at some point during past rehearsals had the opportunity of wearing the crown. I thought, or hoped, that there was something to Pommie's theory.

I was nevertheless hurt. When we got back to the Britannia that evening just after eleven o'clock, we were told that if any girls who were not quite happy with their performances would like to go to the Albert Hall in the morning and rehearse on their own, they were welcome to do so. Only six of the fifty-eight girls put their hands up: Miss New Zealand, Miss Malaysia, Miss Canada, Miss Ireland, Miss Venezuela and me. With tears of disappointment on my cheeks, I practised walking in front of the full-length mirror in Pommie's room until well after curfew as she and my chaperone, Mrs. Protain, were deep in sleep. I finally crept down the fire escape to my own cold room at one in the morning.

I was up and dressed by eight thirty, determined to show these pageant people that they could prejudge all they wanted: I was going to do everything in my power to reach the finals. I was a little surprised at my attitude. I am not an especially competitive person, and I was not a professional pageant entrant. I only entered the Miss Grenada contest because I had been asked. It was the first time it had been held, and it was a big deal for our tiny island. The board of tourism was involved. I felt almost a civic duty to participate and, once I won, to represent Grenada as best I could. It is true that I told a cheering crowd at my departure, "I will leave no stone unturned. I shall do my best to return with the Miss World crown." But I didn't intend it as a prediction. It seemed the right thing to say in the moment. I had been more excited about returning to London, where I had trained with the BBC, than I was by the thought of winning the Miss World title. But here I was on the morning of the pageant, fully engaged.

The bus transported us around Hyde Park to the southwest end of Albert Hall at nine thirty. The BBC crews, preparing for what would be their highest-rated program of the year, were bustling around with their cameras and lights, working from scaffolding and rigs, sipping coffee to keep warm. The Albert Hall was always bitterly cold. The stage appeared ready for the evening and the six of us took turns walking to the marks left for us on the floor. It might seem a simple thing to walk across a stage; but, again, this one was enormous, and there were various raised rostrums or platforms on it of different sizes and heights, so one was always stepping up and stepping down, turning this way and that, meeting one camera here and another there. We were also to stop, pose and smile at specific points.

After each of us had walked the length of the stage about three times, the other girls felt they had done enough. It had taken about a half hour. I asked for permission to stay a little longer. The other girls went back in the bus, and I continued to practise my walk, getting a feel for the stairs, memorizing both their number and the distance between them. I practised walking with my head erect, not looking down at my feet as I stepped from mark to mark. I wanted to give the impression of gliding across the stage.

I was so engrossed in what I was trying to achieve that the sound of a man's voice startled me. It was Lionel Blair, the famous actor and dancer, who would perform during the broadcast. "That's right," he said. "Practice is the only way. I work by that motto." By the time I returned to the hotel, two hours later, I felt ready. Now, on the way back to Albert Hall, I was still ready.

We were in our own little bubble on the bus, the contestants and our minders. There was a murmur of low conversation, suggesting that we were all somewhat anxious. I practised my yoga, deep breathing whenever I started to feel nervous. I was determined to remain calm, take my time and not be rushed or flustered by anyone at this last minute.

In my mind, I was strategizing over all the possible questions Michael Aspel, the compère, or master of ceremonies, might ask me during the contest and how I would handle them. I wanted to appear spontaneous and answer appropriately, even wisely. Pommie and I had often discussed that while I was entering a beauty pageant, beauty was not the only thing on display. All the contestants were beautiful in their own ways. How could the judges possibly compare them, feature for feature, and determine that one was most beautiful? And if they could do such a comparison, I did not see how I could win. I would not be the most beautiful girl on the stage. So we spoke of the need to present what we called "the package," a combination of beauty, grace, poise and intelligence. I worked on my answers.

The streets outside our bus were busy, the end of a cold and wet day, and as we approached the Royal Albert Hall there were obvious signs of a disturbance. Policemen surrounded the building, and a line of demonstrators stretched for nearly a block. They had placards that read "Cattle Market," "Mecca and Morley are Pigs," and "All for a Pound of Flesh." The mood on the bus changed.

One of the first things I had been asked by a reporter on landing in the United Kingdom was my opinion on women's liberation. The question was not unexpected. Women's liberation was an international issue at the time, and it was something I had thought about. I told the reporter that I was conscious of the fact that women needed more opportunities, that we should, by right, be granted more opportunities, and I pointed out that times were changing— there was a woman sitting as governor of Grenada. The truth was that, for me, the pageant was itself an opportunity: I viewed it as a chance to have an experience, one that might lead to something more, whether or not I won.

As for "cattle markets," I didn't really understand the allusion. It seemed to me a stretch, an exaggeration, and the anger of the women outside our bus seemed to me radical. I had nothing against them, or their movement, but I thought there must be better ways to promote the cause. We were all aware that a BBC truck had been bombed in the night by some self-styled anarchists sympathetic to the feminists' cause. It had been all over the news, and the pageant organizers had worried that their star host, the American comedian Bob Hope, would now refuse to appear.

As the bus passed the line, protesters rushed at us with their banners and placards: "We Are Not Ugly, We're Angry," "You Poor Cows," "Miss World, Man's World." Some of them pounded with clenched fists on the sides of the bus. Others were pushing hard, trying to shake the coach. At one point they all started singing, "We Shall Overcome."

We sat there, in our makeup and hairdos, looking out at the rampage. I had never really followed the Miss World pageant before or seen it on television. It was dawning on me what a big deal it must be to raise such a ruckus. Some contestants sang along with the protesters, defiantly, but several were obviously frightened. There had been a bomb, and now this. It was unsettling.

The Mecca men aboard did their best to keep us all calm, reassuring us that there was an abundance of security in place and that police had matters in hand. When the bus came to a complete stop, the doors flew open. We gathered our things and rushed out into the night, the rain, the noise and confusion. The fun, the drama and the history-making were only beginning.

CHAPTER ONE

Tomboy

THE DAY I WAS BORN, our neighbour Miss MacLeish was the one to tell my sister and brother.

"Your Mummy had a little girl today," she said to Pommie and Christopher.

"That must be the limit," was Christopher's reply. He was right.

I was the last of five. My two elder sisters, Pommie and Aileen, were twelve and eleven years older, Christopher was seven years older and Robin four years my senior. Our home was above my father's office at 13 Church Street, St. George's, Grenada. It was a large house, four stories high, overlooking the harbour.

St. George's is the capital of Grenada, a beautiful little city, arranged in the shape of a horseshoe around one of the world's most perfect, natural deep-water harbours. Its red-tiled buildings climb from the shoreline back into the hills, and while I was growing up, many of the streets were still paved with cobblestones. Beyond the hills is a landmass of just 120 square miles, Grenada, the Isle of Spice, population at the time just under one hundred thousand. At its heart is highly productive agricultural land, providing just the right amounts of heat, share and moisture to grow nutmeg, cocoa and bananas, the exports that support the local economy.

Because our house had only a small back garden, we spent much of our time as children looking out the window to the goings-on at Sparrow Hayling's tailor shop or at Miss Margaret's flat above the shoemaker's on Grenville Street. It was a very close-knit community. The children played together, and the maids gathered, speaking patois so we could not understand what they said. The clocks of the three large churches positioned at either end and in the middle of Church Street reminded everyone of the time, on the hour and half hour, day in and day out.

Chrissie Nurse, our nanny, looked after all the Hosten children. She taught us to make bird nests with grass and took us for walks to the fort. It was not unusual to hear her say: "Miss Pommie, don't do that. Your Mummy and Daddy would not approve."

In fact, we could always explain our actions to our mother. It was my father who would disapprove. Everyone who knew him understood that he was a disciplined man who believed in rules. To us, he was simply fussy. The neighbours could always tell when he was not on the island as they could see us children running around the neighbourhood with bare feet. Father always insisted on shoes and socks.

He was a member of the island's professional class, a prominent lawyer who served as president of the Grenada Bar Association and on the town council and was chancellor of the Anglican Church. He had grown up in the countryside, riding a donkey to school before studying law in England. My mother was born in Toronto and emigrated to Grenada with her family at age five. Her family, like my father's, believed in education. She became a teacher, and her brother, Sidney, became the first governor general of St. Vincent and the Grenadines.

Much of our lives revolved around my father's rules and habits. He used to swim at about six thirty every morning, at a beach house he had built about two kilometres out of town on a private beach. He would swim five minutes out, come straight back, rub himself down and go to work. You could not talk to him about anything in the morning. He was always practising, in his mind, for court. You would hear him talking to himself, rehearsing arguments. If you had questions for him, better to wait until evening.

We would sometimes accompany father on these swims but more often on weekends than weekdays. Another part of his routine was his Saturday morning visit to the fish market, and we would frequently join him there too. Dressed in his usual grey pants, supported by braces, and a grey felt hat, he knew most of the vendors by name and they knew him. "Good morning, Mr. Hosten," they would say. "We have your fish right here for you." Jacks were his favourite fish. In the country parishes where he grew up, jacks were served with green figs, plantain and rice, potatoes or breadfruit. Another favourite food was "tight bread" and sweet potato pudding, or "pone," as some people called it. Father would also pick up at least one roast of meat before we returned home.

My first school was Miss Lottie Aird's school in the centre of St. George's. My mother would say goodbye to me in the morning and watch me walk along Grenville Street to Mr. Salfarlie's shop, where I met his daughter Maureen, and the two of us, holding hands, walked the rest of the way together. On one occasion I looked back to wave to my mother, only to find that she had disappeared from the kitchen window. When I returned home later in the day, she noticed that I was distant with her.

"You left the window before I got to school," I said.

My mother laughed and explained that someone had phoned, and she had gone to answer the call. I suppose I had grown accustomed to her attentions, and I enjoyed them.

Mother liked to say that I had "the biggest, roundest, brownest eyes you ever saw, and they missed nothing." She was also impressed at my composure from an early age. One day, when she had been sewing and gone off to do something else, I sat down at her sewing machine and managed to drive the large needle into my left index finger. "Come, Mummy," I said calmly. She returned, witnessed my predicament and gently reversed the direction of the needle. As she did so, the needle which had pinned down my finger came out and a large drop of blood emerged. I never cried. My mother remembered that I smiled with delight at the big red drop.

I was not a squeamish child. I was something of a tomboy, the kind who taught local boys how to bait a hook with a worm. I loved to fish. I often took my makeshift fishing pole and a few small- and medium-size hooks and a sinker down to fish off the old post office in the harbour. I fished with worms or a variety of meats—whatever I could find. I learned that fish could be tempted with bread, if you could get the bread to stay on the hook.

My other favourite thing was to hang around with my older sisters and their friends, who were always trying to get me out of the way by claiming they needed privacy. I could usually insinuate myself into the group. If they were getting ready for dances, I would say, "I just want to help," and I would wear them down until Pommie would say, "Okay, you can help us by making moles." She would hand me a piece of black velvet and a pair of scissors. I had seen them making beauty moles (which were fashionable at the time) before, and I followed their example and cut tiny black circles from the cloth. All the moles went into a small box until the girls were ready to stick them on. I found these preparations fascinating and glamorous.

After Miss Aird's school, I attended the Anglican High School for Girls. There was never any thought of going elsewhere as my parents were staunch Anglicans. The school was run by the Church of England, and Northern Irish nuns taught us. I did reasonably well when I applied myself. I was a strong student in English, and I liked history and the social sciences. I remember studying for the Cambridge School Certificate, which at the time was how a student graduated from high school. One book on the syllabus was George Orwell's *Animal Farm* and another was *High Adventure: Our Ascent of The Everest* by Sir Edmund Hillary. I enjoyed these books immensely.

As indicated by the syllabus and the presence of the Anglican nuns, the island was under British rule. All of us looked to England as the mother country. We were taught to stand at attention to "God Save the Queen" every morning at school (I once amused my parents by bolting out of bed to stand at attention when the anthem was played over the radio in the evening). Most of our news came from the BBC, and the best students aspired to go to university in England. My brother Christopher studied law there, and Pommie trained as a nurse. There were many Brits in administrative positions on the island, in the police force, for instance, and the post office, and these institutions all appeared to function well.

Grenadians at the time were more class conscious than colour conscious. Most of us were of mixed blood. I have African, Scottish and Flemish influences from my father and Scottish and Caribe Indian from my mother. My family taught me that some of the darkest people in Grenada were some of the most respected. The Charles family and the Cromwells were among these. My mother would say, "Miss Charles is a real lady, she would never do such and such." The concept of being mixed race, like Barack Obama or Meghan Markle, did not really exist at the time, at least on our island: you were white or black. No particular privilege attached to either, whereas if you were a member of the professional class, as opposed to working class, you could mix easily at any level of society in Grenada. There was no aristocracy on the island, no social class above the professional class. Because of my father's accomplishments, I never felt like a minority or underprivileged in any way while growing up.

The high school was a few kilometres inland. My friends, Francis McIntyre and Roseanne Murray, whose father was a doctor, would be driven to school by my father in the morning. At lunchtime, the McIntyres would send a car to bring us home and take us back, and at the end of the school we would walk home or sometimes walk partway and then give a few pennies to a boatman to row us across the harbour, which made the journey much more fun.

I was a serious student, studying most evenings. I was still something of a tomboy and had very few boyfriends. Most of the boys I might have gone out with were my brother's friends, which was never going to work. I had more luck with boys who came over on holidays from Trinidad. They would ask you to a movie and sit with an arm around you but that was about it. They were more innocent times.

I once went to a party on a Friday where they were playing music. I was to meet a boy there, and they must have turned the lights down because the next thing I knew was there was a knock at the door and my mother's maid stepped in. "Miss Jenny," she said, "Madam wants to speak to you." I was mortified. When I got home, Mother said simply, "I don't think it's a very safe environment."

It was while I was in high school that a hairstylist in Grenada asked me to model for her. She said she liked working with my cheekbones. She was the first person who ever said anything like that to me. I didn't really know that I had cheekbones before she spoke. I was not focused on myself. But she wanted me for a fashion show, and she wanted to straighten my naturally curly hair, as was popular at the time. She used some chemical, a new product, and my hair started falling out. In chunks. I was distraught. I begged Pommie, who was then in Trinidad, to send me a wig, which she did, and I wore it until my hair came back. It would be some time before I wanted anything to do with modelling again.

CHAPTER TWO

Flying High

I WAS A SELF-STARTER in my teens. Before each vacation period, but especially over Christmas and summer holidays, I would find myself work in a local store or anywhere else they needed extra help. My parents never knew that I was out looking for work. I would arrive home and tell them, "I start at so-and-so next week." I think I impressed them, but that was not why I did it. It gave me something to do over the holidays, and I liked to have some financial independence. When I finished high school at age seventeen, I decided that I wanted to go into broadcasting, which in Grenada meant radio (my family did not have a television until just before I left the island).

I contacted the Windward Islands Broadcasting Service (WIBS) to inquire about positions. Raymond Smith, the chief engineer, told me to send in my curriculum vitae and promised to keep me in mind. A week later, I was called for an interview. I said that I was eager to receive training as a broadcaster and that I was willing to work on a voluntary basis if there were no positions to be filled. I was told there might be a position in the newsroom in a month but that I would need to know how to type.

After the interview, I contacted a local typing school and registered for classes. By the time I was called to the newsroom to replace someone on maternity leave, I was reasonably competent (if slow) on the typewriter. I was treated very well at WIBS, which was a joint venture of the governments of Grenada, Dominica, St. Lucia and St. Vincent. Before long, I was given the opportunity to read children's stories on air, often writing my own tales. The program was called *Kiddies' Corner*. It was successful, and before long I was standing in for some regular broadcasters.

Every year, WIBS sent someone for training at the BBC. I was thrilled to be given this opportunity not long after starting and immediately said I would take it. I loved broadcasting, and radio in particular. I was trained for four or five months in London, after which I managed a secondment to the BBC's Caribbean section. I worked with the journalists and technicians there, not simply chores but going out and doing interviews, and helping them put programs together at a time when all of the content was on big reels of tape that had to be cut and spliced. It was great practical experience.

My position with the Caribbean section ended after I had been in England for a year. I did not feel ready to return home, so I asked for an extension of my leave from WIBS, which was generously granted, and enrolled at Denson Secretarial College at Queen's Gate, not far from the Royal Albert Hall. I wanted to be as well-rounded and qualified as possible to work in news and broadcasting, which meant learning shorthand and improving my typing skills and so on. I lived in a series of rooming houses with other girls and when I finished my courses worked as a secretary to an architect in Hampstead. That got boring after six or seven months, so I wrote my brother in France and asked him to help me find work as an au pair so I could join him there. He did. For another six months, I lived across the English Channel and improved my French, returning to London at Christmas time.

It was not the best of returns. My money had run out. My father had sent me some in the mail, but it was late arriving. I was able to stay with an aunt in a room with coin-operated heating. I had to pawn my little Olympus camera to get enough money to keep the heat on, and I lived on eggs and toast for a few weeks until my father's money arrived. I finally made it home, still not twenty years old.

I returned to WIBS and enjoyed the work, but I was restless. I had met a Canadian broadcaster and mentioned that my mother was Canadian, and he told me that if I ever came to Canada and wanted to work in broadcasting, I should look him up. He gave me his card. I flew to Canada and looked him up and got a low-level job in the bowels of the Canadian Broadcasting Corporation (CBC) in Montreal.

I had always been romantic about Canada because it was my mother's homeland. The reality was less appealing. The job was drudgery. I spent most of my days preparing stock market figures for someone else to read on air. I found the Montreal winter cold and long, and the constant bus strikes did not make it easier—I had no other way to get to work. I also had one terrible experience while I was there.

I had been asked on a date by an actor who was a big deal in Canada at the time. He was not on staff at the CBC, but he worked for the broadcaster. I met him at the CBC offices and he asked me out on a date and I said yes. He took me to his house, a large mansion in which he kept some big dogs. He then proceeded to attack me and tear my top. I pushed him off and insisted on going home, where I had to explain my torn blouse to my roommate. Because the actor was a big deal and not on staff at the CBC, I felt I had no recourse. I did not file a complaint, but I never felt entirely safe in Montreal after that.

Not long afterward, I was invited by a couple of people to a big cocktail party at one of the hotels in Montreal, hosted by British West Indies Airways (BWIA). It was to have Caribbean music and refreshments and it promised to be a good time, so I went and, in the lobby, ran into Bill Otway, a Grenadian who worked in Toronto for BWIA. He saw me speaking French, and I suppose was impressed. He told me that he was hiring people for the airline and asked if I'd be interested. I said I might. A month later, he sent me an application form in the mail. I filled it out and sent it in, and they invited me for an interview. I was offered a position as a flight attendant. It was not a difficult decision: a chance to see the world was much more appealing than another winter in Montreal.

My father was dubious about this new line of endeavour. "You've never had to do that kind of work," he said. "What if you spill coffee on somebody?" I told him I would offer to get their clothes cleaned. He was not convinced. "Are you sure this is for you?" I said, "I'm going to try."

In fact, it was a glorious time to be a flight attendant. We flew to New York at least once a week, to Miami, London, Toronto and all the major Caribbean islands. We had a great crew of flight attendants, and we stuck close together. They are still some of my best friends. We would land in New York and have a crew party or go out to shop. We could live on the travel allowances we were provided and bank our pay, which in those days was reasonably good, and our families were allowed to travel on the airline for free.

People flying with the airline received excellent service. Real meals served on real china with silver cutlery and drinks in genuine glasses. No plastic. Linen tablecloths. And that was in coach. In first class, where I worked most of the time, we heated the rolls before putting them on every tray. As flight attendants, we were required to look our best: carefully groomed in our uniforms with the right shoes, and stockings without ladders. It was all very proper. On flights I served Peter Ustinov, Peter Lawford and his family and Canadian prime minister John Diefenbaker, who was a good friend of my father's later on.

After I'd 'been with BWIA about nine months, the marketing people asked me to pose for a picture or two promoting the airline in my uniform, and I was in posters all over the Caribbean. I also had my photo taken with one particularly noteworthy passenger. I was working in the galley of a Boeing 707 on a flight from Guyana to Trinidad, when two men with cameras slung over their shoulders approached me and asked if they could take my photograph with a tall young lady they pointed out to me. They said they wanted someone in a uniform. "Sure," I said, and went to freshen up. We took the picture.

Later, I took a glass of champagne to the tall young lady, who was sitting in the tourist section of the aircraft. She was Jennifer Evan Wong, the recently crowned Miss Guyana. She was on her way to New York to shop for the Miss World contest. We chatted. She asked me where I was from. I told her. She asked, "Who is Grenada sending to the Miss World?" I said I didn't think they sent anybody: "They're not into that." She said, "They should send you." I laughed.

At the end of every flight, it was the attendants' job to tidy up before the ground crew boarded to do a thorough cleaning. As I was walking through the cabin after the Miss Guyana flight, I noticed a discarded newspaper, *The Grenada Voice*. I popped it in my bag to read at the hotel. When I opened it up, there was an article on the front page announcing that Grenada would send its first representative to the Miss World contest. Quite a coincidence, but I gave it little thought. Two days later, a photo of our two smiling faces made headlines throughout the Caribbean: "Miss Guyana seen with attractive BWIA stewardess, Jennifer Hosten, on flight to Trinidad."

About two weeks later, I was in Grenada for Easter when I bumped into a friend, Gary, in the street. He was helping his mother, Mrs. Gertrude Protain, who was head of the Grenada Tourist Board, to organize the Miss Grenada pageant. "Jen," he asked, "would you be interested in going to the Miss Grenada contest?" I protested that I no longer lived in Grenada. I was based in Port of Spain, Trinidad. He insisted that I was a Grenadian, and that was all that mattered. I told him I would think about it. He said it would be just like a Carnival Queen contest, except the prize would be to go to Miss World, and I promised I would think about it and let him know.

Soon after, Mrs. Protain herself called, asking if I would enter the contest. She had seen the picture of me with Miss Guyana. It would be worth my while, she said, since the winner would receive a wardrobe allowance besides having the opportunity of representing the Isle of Spice at the Miss World pageant. My reply was that I would give the offer serious thought and speak with my sister Pommie, who was my beauty expert.

Gary had mentioned the Carnival Queen contest for a reason. Before I left for Grenada to train at the BBC, I had been talked into entering the annual Carnival Queen contest, which was held during Carnival in February, just before Lent (they've now moved it to August). It was not a beauty contest. It was based more on costume, and I did not win. I came second. My prize as runner-up was to represent Grenada at a Miss Caribbean contest in Antigua. I had attended with my sister Pommie. I did not win there, either. I came second. I think Miss St. Lucia won. Anyway, that was the extent of my experience with this sort of event.

I contacted Pommie, who, by then, had her own spa in Port of Spain at the Trinidad Hilton. It was the first health club on the island, and I had loaned her some money to get it started. I knew she would succeed, and she did. She is a very capable person, and everybody loved her. They called her Nurse Pam. She had her own television program in Trinidad called *Nurse Pam's Program*, which focused on health. She was always glamorous and up on the latest trends, and I would need her help. I was always travelling to

New York and shopping at Bloomingdale's, but she was much better versed in fashion than I was. She cheerfully agreed to assist me.

There were two essential requirements for the Miss Grenada contest: a bathing suit and an evening dress. Pommie and I went on a little shopping spree in Trinidad. The first store on our list was a small boutique in Port of Spain. It was run by an Italian lady with a wonderful sense of style. She showed us her latest collection of bathing suits, and because of my natural light brown complexion, my attention was taken by a French one-piece suit. It was white with panels of flesh-coloured mesh on the sides that give it a see-though effect, while keeping it within the strict rules of the contest.

The search was now on for the evening dress. This had to be distinct, unusual enough that no other competitor would have anything like it. We found just what we needed at another small boutique near the beach. With these two purchases in hand, I felt confident enough to contact the Grenada Tourist Board and say that I would be happy to take part in the Miss Grenada contest. BWIA agreed to give me time off to prepare for and attend the pageant (the preliminaries and the final were two weeks apart), figuring it would be good publicity for the airline.

CHAPTER THREE

Miss Grenada

THE PRELIMINARIES OF THE Miss Grenada contest were held in one of the newest hotels in the seaside resort area of Grand Anse. It was a beautiful setting, and the twelve contenders, including me, paraded around a swimming pool under the stars while the many onlookers sipped drinks and made their own choices. They selected me and four others to be in the finals, to be held at the Regal Cinema in St. George's.

A majestic blue and white building, the Regal Cinema was the largest and most spacious cinema in the capital, with seating capacity of about seven hundred. All of my immediate family were available to assist me, including my sister Pommie and my brother Robin, who came backstage to help. I believe I was a favourite with the crowd from the outset. I could hear my name being chanted as I paraded first in my bathing costume and then in evening wear.

On-stage interviews between the master of ceremonies and individual contestants were an important factor in the contest judging. With this in mind, I had taken time to think of all possible questions and answers so that I had a ready reply when I was asked, "Miss Hosten, if you had to represent our Spice Island abroad, what would you say about Grenada?" I answered: "I would say that Grenada is a combination of all the good things of the other islands with just a little more spice added." My answer was well received, and from then on, I could tell from the reaction of the crowd, which was quite critical of some girls, that I was doing well.

After a relatively long wait for the judges to make their decision, the five of us were asked to reappear onstage, and I felt my knees go weak when I heard my name declared Miss Grenada. The crown was placed upon my head and a microphone handed to me. I could hear myself say I would do my very best to be a good ambassadress when I went abroad to represent my island in just ten weeks.

After a photography session the day after the contest, I was back at work. A good thing, I told myself, to keep my mind off what was ahead of me. The Miss Grenada title brought me an allowance of three thousand dollars to help with my wardrobe and two round-trip tickets to England. I convinced Pommie to accompany me. I knew her help would be invaluable. Meanwhile, I spent as much time as I could sitting in the sun to improve my tan, exercising at a health club, taking saunas and getting massages. Our plan was to fly to London via New York, where we could do some shopping.

The expression "a bad beginning makes a good end" must contain some element of truth. Pommie had brought two suitcases of clothes with her from Trinidad to Grenada but forgot the keys necessary to unlock them. She arranged for them to be sent over, but they would not arrive until the morning of our departure. Pommie had to dress for our flight at the airport, moments before we were to board. What with the goodbyes from members of the Miss Grenada Committee, my parents and others, we began our journey somewhat out of breath. Mrs. Protain of the tourist board, who had decided at the last minute to make the trip, kept us company.

We were three days in New York and spent far too much money on clothes. This was the season of mini and midi dresses, and my old wardrobe was almost obsolete. We did most of our shopping at two well-known New York business houses, Bloomingdale's and Alexander's, where we found most of what was required. The coat that I chose was a real beauty. It was a copy of one in a recent Dior collection, beige with an unusual collection of fasteners in front, and the hood could be pulled up or left to hang at the back.

Fortunately, we had good contacts in Manhattan. Our days were full, and we were wined and dined each evening. At the end of our third day, we were sent off in a most royal fashion. A large group, comprising friends and relatives of Mrs. Protain's, waved until we finally disappeared into the plane. The hostess was given three large orchids of different colours, which she put in the cooler of the VC10 aircraft, along with her instructions to assist us in pinning them on before we disembarked in London.

On our arrival at Heathrow, we were met by a stocky, red-faced gentleman with blonde hair. He had pleasant blue eyes that said quite plainly that he was a friendly, open type of person. Mrs. Protain recognized him from a photograph that had been sent to the tourist board. His name was Peter Jolly, and it suited him. He helped us through the usual immigration and customs proceedings, after which we piled into two Hillman cars parked just outside the exit of the airport. Our baggage handler had not seen the Handle with Care label on the top of a basket, which until then had been carried by Mrs. Protain. He carelessly threw it into the boot of the car, along with the rest of the luggage. We all heard the sound of broken glass. The sweet scent of rum permeated the air. The handler could not apologize enough, but Mrs. Protain was too upset to accept his regrets. We had an unusually quiet drive in from the airport.

We arrived three-quarters of an hour later at the Britannia Hotel in Berkeley Square. There was some confusion at check-in. Pommie and Mrs. Protain were told, after much ado, that they would have to share a room on the top floor above my room. We were given fifteen minutes, just time enough to go to our rooms and freshen up, before we were ushered to the reception room where we were introduced to select members of the Miss World Committee and, after that, various newspaper reporters who peppered me with questions:

"Where is Grenada?"

"What are the natural resources of the island?"

"What is your present ambition, and what are your hobbies?"

"Do you believe in women's liberation?"

"What made you enter this contest?"

My previous experience in the broadcasting field must have been a great asset. I can remember only one other girl, Miss Sweden, who was unruffled by the press. She, too, had worked in journalism. Even Julia Morley, Eric's wife and head of the organizing committee, who should have had considerable experience with the press, would prove in the days ahead to be so anxious at the prospect of an interview as to be rendered unwell.

The press took a number of pictures that day, including a couple of me in the lotus position. I had mentioned that yoga was a hobby. That evening we were encouraged to dine in the hotel dining room, and I'm glad we did. I was amazed by the waiters, who seemed to have gathered from every corner of the globe: not only Italy, France and Spain but as far away as Persia. This cosmopolitan staff would be a blessing during our stay for many of the girls, especially those exhausted by gallant efforts to speak the English language and relieved to find someone who understood their own.

The pageant supplied one chaperone for every three girls. The chaperones were supposed to speak the languages of their girls, and sincere efforts were made; but an English accent is difficult to overcome, and many meanings were lost to improper pronunciation even when the sentences were formally correct. Hilary was the name of my chaperone, and a more delightful girl one could not hope to know. We chatted often. I learned that she was engaged to be married to a doctor and wished her luck.

My first roommate was a girl from Gambia. She seemed pleasant but distant and not particularly outgoing. She was much happier when an old friend of hers arrived from Ghana. They apparently knew each other quite well before and now spent a great deal of time together. Miss Gambia later moved into a room with another friend (Miss Nigeria) and a third representative from Africa (there was a shortage of rooms). Miss Malaysia, a late arrival, moved in with me.

The first big evening function of pageant week was held at a private club. This took the form of a cocktail party during which the girls were introduced by country in alphabetical order. Each girl was interviewed by the MC and asked to say a few words to the gathering, which also included members of the press. I noticed that all the girls said more or less the same thing, although sometimes in different words. They were happy to be in England, they were having such a marvellous time, they were impressed at the hospitality of the English. It did not always sound sincere. When I heard my name announced, I turned unconsciously to my sister for some moral support, but she was not where I had thought she would be. There was no time for regret. Up onstage I went, dressed in a striking red and black dress, the material of which had come from the House of Dior.

In response to the master of ceremonies, I said, "Like everyone else, I am delighted to be here and quite honoured to have been chosen to represent my little Island of Grenada, not to be confused with Granada, that town in Spain." I then recited for them a short poem, "Ode to Grenada," written for me by my mother, the English tutor:

> An ocean pearl, a nutmeg seed,
> Atom, acorn, teardrop,
> All small things.
> So is that far-off sunny land
> From where I come and call it home.
> An emerald, set in diamond and turquoise,

To see is to believe.
And then to come to live and love that
Caribbean gem, the Isle of Spice.

Maybe it was my imagination, but I swear I could see some tears in the eyes of the audience. I was later told that I won some people over that night.

By the time I got back to my hotel, I had a better idea of what I'd got myself into with the Miss World pageant. There was intense competition among the girls to get in front of the cameras. The more aggressive candidates were always encroaching on more timid girls, who preferred to step back rather than be stepped on. The organizers had set us up to battle one another in this way, encouraging us to do anything to get our pictures in the papers. Although I was not of an aggressive nature, I tried to hold my own. It was not easy. It was clear to me that the cameramen for the British news media shared a certain attitude toward the girls. In past years, only contestants of very fair complexion had been crowned Miss World. The photographers, therefore, made no apologies for taking many more pictures of the English and Scandinavian girls.

I put in a call to the front desk to be awakened by six. There was a heavy schedule of rehearsals and events for us every day of pageant week. I know that many girls awoke at seven or even seven thirty, before our departure from the hotel by eight; but I was determined to be well groomed on every occasion, and I felt more at ease when I did not have to rush. I kept my wake-up call at six all week, and Pommie, too, would awaken early in her room on the floor above, put on her dressing gown and come down to my room by way of the fire escape (she did not want to encounter anyone in the elevator without proper attire) to help me dress.

CHAPTER FOUR

The Miss World Pageant

ERIC MORLEY, HEAD OF MECCA PROMOTIONS, was about five foot eight with black hair, greying at the temples. He had the physique of a man who liked his beer and bowed legs that gave him a duck-like walk. The first thing one noticed about him, however, was his watery eyes and constant blinking. As the founder of the Miss World pageant, he was obviously an important figure to all of us, but his abrasive manner did not endear him to the girls.

Mecca was a family business. Julia Morley, Eric's wife, breezed into the reception room at the hotel some two days after our arrival. Although tall and assertive, she seemed shy when she spoke and had a nervous habit of brushing her pin-straight black hair from her face. She had met Eric in one of his dance halls in 1960 and never wanted us to forget that she was his wife: "Hi girls," she would start. "I'm Mrs. Morley."

The crew brought into work on the Miss World contest consisted of many other Morley family members. Two of Julia Morley's sisters and two of her brothers did everything from answering phones to preparing seating plans and occasionally filling in for chaperones. A nephew was responsible for rounding up the girls. (Eric Morley et al. left Mecca in the late seventies over a dispute with its parent company, and Eric died of a heart attack in 2000; but Julia still runs the pageant, and the family is connected to the global *Dancing with the Stars* franchise, thanks to Eric's role in its earlier iterations.)

One of the organizers who most interested the girls was George Anderson, a short man in his late fifties with jet black hair. He had been seconded from Mecca's head offices on Southwark Street to handle public relations and other duties for the pageant. He was a favourite with the girls after endearing himself to us by being the only member of Mecca with any time to attend to the needs of the chaperones from abroad, giving them details of coming events and getting them tickets for the many formal functions. We all took turns guessing at his origins. It was finally discovered that he was Danish.

Mecca Leisure, the corporate entity through which the pageant was run, was one of Britain's largest entertainment companies. Founded during the Great Depression, it had expanded to include dance halls, nightclubs, hotels, bingo parlours, catering and theme parks across the United Kingdom. Jimmy Savile, the once-popular (later-disgraced) disc jockey and TV presenter, had managed a couple of Mecca dance halls. The DJ and record producer Pete Waterman was another Mecca personality. Not all the company's facilities were first class—some, in fact, were quite dingy, as I would learn—but it was a successful business at the time.

Our mornings began with roll call. We were addressed by our countries rather than our names and were afterward herded into the buses for rehearsals at Royal Albert Hall. Julia Morley's brother, Harvey, was in charge of getting us there, but Eric ran us through our paces. On the first occasion, all fifty-eight of us sat in the audience section on the right-hand side of the auditorium, waiting and watching as he called us, one at a time, to the stage with its six raised platforms covered in white vinyl and joined to each other by steps—three steps down from the first platform to the second, two steps up to the next one and so on.

"Miss Greece, Miss Greece, where is that dizzy-headed girl? Will someone send Miss Greece up to the stage?" Morley yelled. He was always addressing us in his characteristic pose, legs apart, stomach extended. He was sarcastic and exacting, bent on playing the role of lord and master. From time to time, he would put the crown on his head and walk around the stage as an example to us. Many of the girls were afraid of him. It would have been a bad thing to get on his wrong side.

"Well, Miss Greece, and just what do you think you are doing? If you think you have a chance of winning this contest, you had better think again," he continued. Miss Greece, who seemed slightly slow, was trying in vain to follow Morley's instructions onstage. In desperation, he called for Miss Guyana, who was next in line.

Miss Guyana, of Eurasian descent, did not smile much. She walked with military precision to her positions and looked tall onstage, but she would have been even more impressive if she had projected her personality. Nevertheless, she followed instructions, and one could see that she was a favourite of Morley's. In fact, by the second rehearsal it was plain to see that Morley had already done his own judging and that she was high on his list.

I was the next called, and I can still hear the voice of Morley shouting, "Miss Grenada." Heart pounding, I walked as confidently as possible onstage, aware of the many eyes upon me. It was unnerving, even though I had felt all along that I was well liked by the contestants and also the chaperones. They were always willing to come to my aid. As I now stepped from one platform to the other, I tried to make it down the steps with only the slightest glance at them. It was difficult, not least because my eyes were watering and felt as though they had sand in them (more about this later).

I got through my steps and made a sketch of the stage, estimating the distance and the number of steps between each platform. I watched the other girls try to follow Morley's instructions and often felt for them: there were definite language problems. So few of the contestants spoke English, and Morley did not have the patience to deal with them. He would shout at them, which only made the girls more anxious and caused him to lose his voice.

Some days we rehearsed until early evening (the last two days until ten o'clock). Other days, the lot of us were taken to places of special interest in London for our own benefit, and for that of the media. I almost wished that I had not been so fortunate to have seen most of them during my previous time in England. We saw the House of Parliament and Madame Tussauds. It was at the latter that I again spoke to Miss Guyana. She was genuinely surprised to see me among the contestants rather than on a plane. I noticed a change in her. She had seemed very young and friendly when we first met on board the airliner; she now appeared mature and very confident. The press, in fact, seemed to pick up on her confidence and Morley's favouritism. They were soon singling her out for more than her share of photographs.

One morning, fifteen contestants, including me, were awakened at a quarter to six. The publicity men had been up all night devising a plan for fifteen girls to perform an outdoor workout in shorts and woollen vests, in front of photographers, of course. The venue was Grosvenor Square, and from the moment we arrived, the whole thing seemed ridiculous. It was the coldest day since our arrival, and it began to drizzle. We took our positions on the wet grass. Pearl Jansen, Miss Africa South, a lovely girl of black and Indian heritage, was put at the head of the exercise class. She was a games teacher in South Africa and comfortable in the role.

Pearl and I had bonded early in the week. As we watched for the sign to begin, I recalled my pleasant first meeting with her and her

African chaperone. Afterwards, she had come up to me and said, "Miss Grenada, I think that you are the sweetest girl here. If I do not win the contest, I want you to win."

"That is very kind of you, Pearl," I answered. "I return your compliment." And I meant it.

The expressions of satisfaction on the faces of the photographers indicated that the exercise session was coming off well despite the cold and damp. My mood improved as we began to move and warm up. In fact, before long I was looking around at the green park and the leaves just beginning to fall, and the world seemed beautiful. To be safe, Pommie insisted I take a hot bath when I got back to the hotel and helped to give me a towel rub to encourage circulation and combat any virus I might have picked up as a result of this early morning escapade.

Health was a constant concern for the contestants. The last thing anyone wanted was a cold or a fever or a rash. My own health problem, the feeling of sand in my eyes, was my own fault. Before leaving the Caribbean, I had sat for many days in the sun to ensure a perfect tan. Being already of an olive brown complexion, I tan to a golden bronze, and I was determined to reach just that shade on the eve of the contest. In those days, we helped the process along with Johnson's baby oil and iodine, which is terrible for the protection of your skin, but it does get you dark. Unfortunately, my tan began to peel and fade not long after my arrival in England, where there was little or no sun. My sister made enquiries about the rental of a sun lamp and found one.

One evening, I went to my sister's room and sat in front of the lamp. Pommie handed me a pair of sunglasses to put on but not realizing how important these were to the whole process, I took them off while we chatted. After about twenty-five minutes, I began to feel discomfort in my right eye. Pommie suggested that I had had enough "sun" for that evening.

I returned to my room on the floor below by way of the fire escape and went to bed. At about one o'clock, I awoke with the feeling that there was sand in my eyes. My pillow was bathed in tears, and I could not open my eyes, much less see. I bore the pain until five o'clock when, unable to stand it any longer, I called Pommie on the telephone, trying my best not to waken Miss Malaysia across the room.

Pommie was not surprised to find that I could not sleep. She, too, had been affected by the lamp. She had sat close enough to get burns on her face. We were anxious not to let anyone else find out what had happened. I did not want the sun lamp to find its way into the newspapers. How could we explain that an already coloured girl had got burned trying to obtain a better tan under a lamp? We found the house doctor who declared that I was lucky not to have damaged the delicate tissues of my eyes. He prescribed drops, which had to be taken every four hours.

Our cover story was that I had developed an allergy in my left eye. As happens at pageants, the publicity men quickly set about trying to pitch this story to the newspapers. One of them found three eye patches decorated with sequins, one red, one black and one yellow. Monty, a photographer from one of the newspapers, was called in for the "scoop." He took several pictures of me with the patches but told us afterwards that he had been unable to convince his editor that I had, in fact, developed an allergy. It was probably for the best.

I had more luck with another publicity stunt. British Overseas Airways Corporation (BOAC; now British Airways) wanted to use some of us girls in our national costumes in a newspaper ad. Grenada did not have a traditional national costume so I had decided to make one. The idea for it was taken from a painting by the Grenadian artist John Benjamin and constructed by Trinidad's Carlyle Chang, who had a studio on Dundonald Street in Port of Spain. Pommie and I had told him what we were looking for and he executed it beautifully.

The result was a play on the nutmeg, Grenada's primary export. I was to be the centre of the fruit, encased in a yellow pod with large green leaves on the outside. It was an elaborate, imaginative design with accessories made of beaten copper, Chang's signature. It came with a specially constructed packing case to hold its shape. Before packing it up, I tried it on three times so I could get used to assembling it and carrying its considerable weight.

My costume passed BOAC's test, and I was chosen to be in the advertisement. I was delighted, and proud for Grenada. Others to be photographed were Miss New Zealand, Miss Nicaragua, Miss Canada, Miss Guyana and Miss Jamaica. We were driven to a tiny studio in Chelsea and at the top of a long flight of stairs greeted by the photographer and his assistant. We changed one at a time in the cramped facilities and had our hair styles touched up by a young hairdresser named Martin Samuels. I was impressed with his quick ability and quietly asked him if he would do my hair for the finals. He said he would be happy to, so I got his phone number and told him I would call to arrange an appointment.

The BOAC ad was a great success. The picture did everyone justice and boosted our spirits, and my makeshift national costume had its moment in the sun. If the sun lamp gave me my worst moments that week, the costume provided one of the best. In between were a lot of curious, if not eye-popping, incidents that gave me my first taste of the big-time pageant business.

CHAPTER FIVE

Behind the Curtain

URING REHEARSALS, WE WERE ALLOWED a coffee break at eleven o'clock. We would saunter into a small room fitted up as a bar, where a large woman with a ruddy Irish complexion served coffee and cakes. It was during these breaks that the girls got the opportunity of talking to each other, and often about each other. One of my favourites was Miss Israel. She was a tall, slim blonde whom I found sincere and thoughtful. Miss France was another outstanding girl both in appearance and manner, and she had that certain French finesse. She told me point-blank that most of the girls lacked class. "It is a great pity," she said, "a great pity."

Miss Australia, Vali Kemp, was a favourite with the news media. Among the girls, however, she was the least popular. She seemed solely concerned with herself. It was rumoured that she awoke each morning at five to wash and set her hair, which was long, black and thick. Everyone said that she wore at least two hairpieces, a statement she vehemently denied.

Another girl who had a difficult time was Miss United Kingdom, Yvonne Ormes. She had a lot going for her, being the hometown favourite and an attractive blonde. What was unusual this year,

however, was that Miss United Kingdom was being snubbed. I personally liked her but thought perhaps she appeared too sedate or
uninterested to be a true favourite. It did not help her that the contestants from Greece, Ireland and Gibraltar showed their jealously
by forcing their way into her picture-taking sessions. She was not
the type to stand up to them.

It did nothing to improve the sense of conviviality among the girls
that newspapers were posting odds on who would be crowned Miss
World. The people in England wagered heavily on the contest. It had
never occurred to me that betting would be permitted, and it seemed
to be a revelation to the rest of the girls as well. We learned that the
Miss World pageant is one of the big chances of the year for bookies
to make money, next only to Ascot and other high-stakes horse races.

When I first arrived in London, I was placed among the first
twelve girls in terms of popularity and potential. Three days before
the finals, the newspapers put my odds at twenty-five to one. In
other words, I was a long shot. Miss Sweden, Miss Australia and
Miss Norway were among the favourites.

One day, we were told that a surprise was in store for us: the
popular singer Engelbert Humperdinck was coming to pay us a visit.
Humperdinck had been a forgettable lounge singer in the early 1960s
under his real name, Arnold Dorsey. In 1965, he hooked up with
Tom Jones's manager, adopted the name of Engelbert Humperdinck
(the name of a nineteenth-century German composer) and began
to find success. By the time we encountered him, he had enjoyed a
hit on both sides of the Atlantic with "Release Me" and launched
a television show on ABC in the United States. He was one of the
more popular entertainers in the world.

We gathered to be presented to Engelbert in the reception lounge
of the hotel. Halfway through the introductions, there was a commotion, and all eyes turned to Miss Austria, who was being escorted
out of the room by a member of the Mecca staff. The incident started

tongues wagging. We soon heard the reason for her forced departure: she had been wearing a sheer blouse with nothing underneath. The photographers noticed and naturally gave her their full attention. The next morning's newspapers featured the headline: "Miss Austria Sent to Room to Put on Bra."

For reasons none of us understood, Mecca decided to reply to the newspaper article, claiming that Miss Austria had not been braless: it had only seemed that way. In any event, Miss Austria was noticeably absent from our evening functions. The story went that she was running off to meet Engelbert.

The reporters did their best to put girls on the spot with tricky questions, especially on such issues as race and women's liberation. The early 1970s were the height of the anti-Apartheid movement, a protest against enforced segregation and the unspeakably cruel racist policies of the South African government, and the ensuing controversy had caught up with the pageant. Reporters were asking why South Africa was entering only one white contestant in Miss World. Mecca had tried to address the issue by arranging two contestants from South Africa. One, white, was called Miss South Africa. The other, Pearl Jansen, was black and called Miss Africa South.

Most contestants were careful and gave evasive answers to difficult questions. Miss Sweden who, again, was a journalist, was outspoken, if undiplomatic, in her answers. She made comments to the effect that she was fed up with the chauvinism of the whole scene. She seemed to agree that Eric Morley was exploiting us and was quoted as saying that she felt "just like a puppet. I don't even want to win. If I were not under contract to the organizers, I would walk out at once." That may have been responsible for some members of the press turning somewhat against Morley, and it may have hurt Miss Sweden's chances.

I had felt from the moment of our arrival in England that we were under surveillance of some kind. Wherever we went, there were onlookers present, taking notes. At one early photographic session, we were required to pose in a large group with bathing suits on. Afterward, the media had a field day, with photographers snapping candid pictures of particular girls and various radio stations (mainly from the BBC Overseas Network) recording interviews. I spoke with the Caribbean Service and a freelance reporter for Radio Guyana, not a great deal of attention, but my interviews went off without a hitch. As they came to an end, I caught sight of an odd couple in the background. They were smiling and had obviously been listening to what had been said.

A fellow from Ceylon (now Sri Lanka), who was a friend of the Ceylonese representative, sauntered over to me and asked, "Miss Grenada, aren't you?"

"Yes," I replied.

"What do you think of this whole business?"

"What business?" I asked.

"Don't you think that racial prejudice exists in the running of this contest?" he said.

I asked him why he thought this.

"Well, just look at how much more attention is given to Miss Sweden and Miss Austria. You are every bit as attractive as they are, and yet here you sit alone."

There was some truth in what he said. One need only look at the list of previous Miss World winners, heavy with representatives from the Netherlands, Scandinavia, the United Kingdom and Austria, to know that it was uphill for girls of colour. In my heart, I tended to agree with this fellow, but I had decided on arriving in London that I was going to take the high road in everything I did. I thought poise and tact would be part of the "package" judges might find appealing at the end of the week. After all, Miss World was not only crowning a new queen: under the terms of the contest, it was essentially hiring the person who would represent the pageant around the world for the next year. So I chose to give a diplomatic answer, emphasizing factors other than race in the judging.

"Well," I replied, "I guess nobody has really heard about Grenada before. After all, this is the first year that we have ever had a representative to this contest. And if some girls are favoured, I think it is a case of personal preference. Gentlemen prefer blondes or something."

At this stage, I noticed the odd couple making notes for the first time. He was a short, grey-haired gentleman, and his companion was a lady with brown hair tied severely in a knot at the back of her head. Her dress was slightly puritanical, and she spoke with a foreign accent. They were supposed to have been members of the press, but they were not conducting interviews or taking pictures with the cameras they carried. (On all the occasions that I would see them—I would look for them after this first incident—they did no journalistic work.) I guessed that they were keeping watch on us and working as some sort of preliminary judges. Anyway, they now seemed in agreement for the first time since I had spotted them, and something told me they were in agreement about me.

The final dress rehearsal, during which I was one of the forty-three girls pushed to the sideline, went disastrously for me. After my morning of practice on the day of the finals, I was in a better mood. I returned to the hotel to find everything in chaos. Harrods Beauty Salon had been contracted to comb the hair of all the girls; but the salon had assigned only six or seven hairdressers to the task, and there were fifty-eight of us. I had visions of half the contestants walking across the stage in the same hairstyle. Fortunately, I had already telephoned Martin Samuels, and he had promised to arrive at the Britannia by four in the afternoon.

One of the organizers' rules was that no one could invite guests to their room. This was perhaps wise with respect to security, but it created problems for my hairdresser. I had asked him to call me from the reception area upon his arrival. He did, and I told him to take the lift to the floor above him. I next called Pommie in her room to alert her. A few minutes later, the two of them burst into my room by way of the fire escape, Pommie leading the way and Martin following, bag in hand. We agreed that his cover story, if caught, was that he was my cousin and he had simply come to wish me well that evening.

Martin tried several styles and finally said, "You know Jennifer, I think you deserve a simple style," and with a few more strokes of the brush I saw what he meant. With the help of a tiny hair piece to add thickness, the effect was that of a cascade of hair. The style suited me as my face is on the small side, and the surrounding hair added dimension. I needed some height on top and told him how much and where. He agreed and carried out the idea like a true artist.

Just as Martin was about to depart, the sound of a knock at the door almost made my heart stop. Miss Malaysia had forgotten her key. She seemed surprised to see Martin in the room but said to me in her delightful Malaysian accent, "It is okay, Jennifer. I don't say anything." Martin escaped safely from the hotel ten minutes later.

My hair in place, Pommie and I rushed to complete our preparations and pack up everything we needed to take to the Albert Hall. It was no small feat of organization to ensure we forgot nothing. Pommie was her usual helpful self and looked particularly lovely in her low-cut black evening gown. She wore long diamante earrings and a matching necklace. The effect was eye-catching.

The bathing suit we packed was the same white number I had worn for the Miss Grenada contest. I had taken to wearing a tiny gold chain around my waist under the suit to add a little more interest—it showed through the sheer mesh panels on the side.

I also packed my secret weapon, a gown I had chosen especially for the competition. The entire creation was made from a rich gold fabric, the perfect colour to complement my complexion. It had a delicate, low-cut bodice crocheted out of thick, shimmering gold strands. My shoulders and upper arms were bare. From the bodice down were the same shimmering gold strands hanging fringe-like down to my ankles (underneath were silky gold harem pants). I wore the gown with long gloves (extending past my elbows) of the same crocheted material as the bodice, and a single large and elaborate gold earring on my right ear. The effect was simplicity, sexuality and elegance, not necessarily in that order. I was confident that it would stand out even in the tough competition of a Miss World contest.

CHAPTER SIX

THE NIGHT
OF NIGHTS

THERE WAS A SPECIAL CONTINGENT of both plain-clothes and uniformed policemen in the area where we disembarked from the bus. We were immediately ushered into the Albert Hall and then through a seemingly endless series of corridors to the dressing room. This was a large space divided by partitions to give more privacy. Large mirrors had been set up in front of bench-like tables for our use, and it was a case of first come, first served.

Just as there had been too few hairstylists available in the afternoon, there were too few tables for all the girls now. The more aggressive contestants talked the less assertive ones into changing tables or giving up their tables. Many of the shy girls stood to apply their final touch-ups and make their quick costume changes. As I was one of the first inside the dressing room, I was able to secure a fairly good table. It took a great effort, however, to keep it.

There were a number of makeup artists there to help the girls and one or two of the Harrods hairdressers. They went from table to table and did what they could between changes. The chaperones held clothes and offered moral support, which was greatly needed at the time. Cups of coffee, tea and orange soft drinks were available from a machine in the waiting room. I had asked for beer and before my first appearance onstage had finished off a Heineken.

Some of my relatives had arrived early. Before things got under-way, I made my way to the backstage area, which was also covered by BBC cameras, and peeked through a tiny crack in the screen to find them. I spotted them sitting in a prominent position on the right side of the large hall in the second balcony row. I felt lucky. Apart from Pommie, I had another sister—Aileen lived in Gloucestershire with her English-born husband and two children—in the audience. They had secured tickets for themselves and many other members of the family. My brother arrived from France on the day of the contest. My uncle on my father's side and his wife had been vacationing in Europe and were also present. A cousin, Anne, had been terribly excited about my entering and because of Aileen's persistence and planning, they all got seats together.

It meant so much to me to have my most ardent supporters, my family, in the hall and as excited as it was possible to be. In addi-tion, I had other supporters in the crowd. Mrs. Protain had secured tickets for her son, Gary, and his girlfriend, Audrey, and many other well-wishers from Grenada. I knew that when I took the stage, I would hear shouts of "Well done, Grenada" and "We're backing you, Jennifer" and feel a boost. The knowledge that one has support in the crowd can be an important factor to anyone on a stage (just as the feeling that an audience is not with you can be devastating). Knowing where my relatives were seated would be a great advantage to me.

Being backstage and without televisions, we did not see a lot of the program that night. The opening for television audiences was a rotating gold crown against a black background so it appeared to be floating in space with an authoritative man's voice saying: "The lure of a crown! Fifty-eight countries from all over the globe have sent beautiful girls to London tonight in search of a title. Ladies and gentlemen, Miss World 1970!"

The opening act was a seven-man modern dance troupe headed by Lionel Blair, whom I had seen at rehearsals that morning, now looking very mod in a double-breasted burgundy jacket over a frilly black shirt and bell-bottom trousers. His dancers scampered about the stage and sang:

> *Is it America, Australia or Mexico?*
> *Is it Gambia? Mauritius? Well, we just don't know.*
> *Liberia, Nigeria or maybe Spain.*
> *There's just a chance Miss Austria might win again...*

At the end of their number, all of us girls came out onstage in our national costumes—Miss America as Uncle Sam, Miss Canada as a Mountie, Miss Seychelles in a grass skirt, me in my nutmeg outfit— for Lionel's grand finale:

> *Miss World! Miss World!*
> *The most beautiful girl in the world!*

We all scurried off stage and hurriedly changed into our evening gowns backstage. In front of the cameras, the judges were introduced, a panel of nine eminences, several of whom the Morleys had rounded up at a Commonwealth meeting that week: the high commissioner of Malawi, the Indonesian ambassador to the United Kingdom, the premier of Grenada, the maharaja of Baroda, the Danish singer Nina, Glen Campbell, BBC personality Peter Dimmock, the British film producer Nat Cohen and the actress Joan Collins, who was then at the height of her career.

I recognized Joan Collins from her role in *Island in the Sun*, a film set in the Caribbean and filmed in Grenada, also starring Harry

Belafonte, Dorothy Dandridge, James Mason and Joan Fontaine. She had struck me as flirty and vivacious. I recalled that Nina had recorded songs with a Caribbean flavour that I had heard on the radio once on a visit to Italy. When I saw that the premier of Grenada was a member of the judging panel, my hopes of making the finals sank. I thought he wouldn't vote for me, even if he thought I deserved it. He would feel obliged not to show favouritism to the contestant from his island. Another reason for my disappointment was that my father had not long before acted on behalf of the British government, which had brought (and won) a case against Eric Gairy for mismanaging funds in his capacity as chief minister of Grenada. As a result of my father's efforts, Gairy had been put out of office. I did not expect he would put that entirely out of his mind even now, several years later, as head of the Grenadian government.

The next event would see us parade, one at a time, across the stage as the announcer said a few words about where we were from, our jobs, our hobbies and so on. This was the short trip that I had practised for so long that morning, and it was perhaps the most critical element of the contest. On this basis alone, the field of fifty-eight would be cut down to fifteen.

As soon as the girls began walking out to take their moments in the spotlight, the audience could start to appreciate the bewildering variety on offer and just how difficult it would be for the judges to make their choices. Some contestants were tall and strapping; others were fine-featured and petite. Every skin and hair colour imaginable was represented. Among the contestants' occupations were model, typist, machinist, student, bank clerk and journalist. Some were in their first pageant; others had won as many as nine beauty contests on the road to this one.

The Mecca attendants were bustling around backstage to ensure that we all paraded out in proper order, alphabetically by country, and that we all wore on our gowns and our wrists the numbers that had been assigned us. Mine was twenty-one, which had been a reasonably lucky number for me in the past. (I remembered winning a raffle of a drum set, complete with cymbals, when I had chosen the number twenty-one at a children's bazaar some ten years before.) It was quite an assembly line behind the curtain. As one Mecca person checked to make sure the next girl got up onstage at the appropriate moment, another Mecca person helped each girl leaving the stage back to the changing room by the quickest route. This chain operation had to be done efficiently because of the limited time allotted to each girl.

Yet another Mecca gentleman caused quite a stir in the dressing room. He was charged with caring for the crown, sceptre and cloak that the winner of Miss World 1970 would wear. A lot of eyes popped out as he passed through the waiting room. The crown was large with a solid gold base under intricate filigree interspersed with various stones and topped by a series of peaks with tiny gold balls. It had been designed only that very year to celebrate the twentieth anniversary of the Miss World contest and was insured reportedly for twenty thousand pounds, but how true that was no one knew. The sceptre was also gold and the kind one usually sees in museums. The cloak, also brand new, was of a rich gold material, with two hook fasteners in the front.

Right before my first appearance onstage, a strange thing happened. I was in my evening grown in the waiting room with Pommie when we noticed Miss Japan and her chaperone looking at me and whispering excitedly. It was only afterwards, at the ball, that I learned that Miss Japan had received a letter from her mother the day before the contest saying that she had had a dream in which a girl with a gold evening dress was crowned Miss World. I was the only girl in gold that evening. Pommie told me she, too, had a dream two days before the contest in which she and others in our family had carried me on their shoulders. At the time, I did not put much stock in dreams. As a child, I had always been told that dreams meant the reverse of what they appeared to mean.

Although I am not a big drinker, I managed to find a second Heineken before going onstage. It helped me relax. I knew how much was riding on this one tour of the stage, less than a minute in length. I had to nail it if I was going to convince the judges that someone from outside of Morley's favourite fifteen deserved to be a finalist. I reviewed my game plan as I stood in the wings. I wanted to come out and say, *Here I am, look at me. I'm not just a dress or a hairdo.* I wanted to interest people, make an impression. It seemed to me that if the judges were looking for a new Miss World, I had to perform as if I already owned the title. I would put myself in character and adopt the regal bearing of a woman already accustomed to the crown.

Making an impression is easier said than done. I had seen in rehearsals the various ways that a girl could fail to put her best self forward. Some forgot to compose their faces, or to smile. Some did not move with confidence: they were stiff or shy or timid, forgetting to move their arms; or taking short, tentative steps; or glancing down at their feet, hiking their gowns before a step up or down. Some even lost their marks and wandered around the stage. Except for wandering around stage, these are small details, but they leave an impression—and they matter hugely when all the judges have to go on is how you move across the stage.

Finally, I came out from behind the curtain into the light at the top of the stage to hear my name called: "Miss Grenada." I walked forward at a casual pace, tummy in, shoulders back, chin up, body relaxed, enjoying the applause. I took the first series of four steps down without looking at them, eyes toward the audience. I stepped nimbly, even eagerly, down them. It helped greatly that my gown was only to my ankles and flowed easily and did not interfere with my changing elevations (some girls wore gowns made to stand in as opposed to walk in).

I posed at the next mark, continuing to look at the audience, thinking of all those people as friends, not as strangers or adversaries. Several times I reminded myself to slow down. I was not going to push myself off the stage or let anyone else hurry me off. It might be the only opportunity I had. Crossing to the next mark, in front of the judges, I stopped and gave them a nod and a genuine smile, still taking my time. I tried to look each member of the panel in the eye. On a flight, I had once met a man who had judged beauty contests in New York and California. He told me that a judging panel is always made of different people from different backgrounds and that they seldom agree on standards of perfect beauty. Rather, he said, the human element is very important: "If you can look good and still maintain your humility and charm, you will stand a good chance." And then I turned for the last part of the walk, moving my arms, and my hips too, not unnaturally but perhaps more than most contestants.

I felt I had done as best I could. Just as I was leaving the stage, a man sitting right up front jumped from his seat, stretched out his arm and handed me what looked like a calling card. It contained his name and address and identified him as a member of the Baltic Press. The card was ripped from my hand by a Mecca handler, no doubt for security reasons. After the contest, I was given the opportunity to read the other side of the card, which said, "YOU are the winner."

When all fifty-eight girls had completed their appearances, we stood in anxious silence for the results of the first elimination, which would take us down to fifteen contestants. I was one of the lucky fifteen. Some girls who had not heard their names called slumped down in their chair, dejected; others said that everything was a fix and that the choices came down to politics; still others seemed relieved at not having to bother with the rest of the competition. Pommie would not let me dwell on the eliminations: "Never mind," she said, "we still have a lot of work ahead of us so let's get cracking."

CHAPTER SEVEN

Stealing the Show

A S WE CHANGED INTO OUR bathing suits backstage, it was Bob Hope's moment to shine. The American actor and comedian, born in London, was almost seventy and had been performing professionally for more than a half century. His best years in motion pictures were behind him; but he was still a regular face on television, and he had carved out a new role for himself with his popular USO tours to members of the US Armed Forces. He also had a long history with beautiful women and the Miss World pageant.

Although married to his wife Dolores since 1934, Hope had a reputation as a womanizer. His biographer, Richard Zoglin, writes that he had "affairs with chorus girls, beauty queens, singers and showbiz wannabes throughout his seventies. He had a different girl on his arm every night. He was still having affairs into his eighties." He had been performing at the Miss World pageant regularly since the 1960s, and each year the winner would join him on his tours to entertain the troops. The story goes that he fell in love with Miss World 1961, and they had an affair. She was a British girl and had gone to live in Hollywood for a while, working as his assistant. Apparently, Mrs. Hope broke that up and kept a close eye on him and future Miss Worlds.

Bob Hope was not at his best that night at the Albert Hall. I don't want to accuse him of mailing it in, but he was reading his jokes from a teleprompter and his material was stale. He was getting no laughs from the London audience. A lot of his punchlines were lost on the audience, and some of those that did land were taken as offensive:

"I'm very happy to be here at this cattle market tonight. Moo. . ."

"Last year I promised Miss World a part in a picture, and I'm going to have to do something about it soon because she's getting tired of all the rehearsals."

"I don't want you to think I'm a dirty old man because I never give women a second thought. My first thought covers everything."

"This was the second time I was invited to Buckingham Palace. I guess they wanted the towels back."

"The closest I ever came to a real princess was meeting Tiny Tim in the dressing room at the YMCA."

He was struggling. The crowd was getting restless, and then all of a sudden, things went from bad to worse. We were backstage so we could not see what was happening in the auditorium, but we could hear a lot of noise. It began with a loud football rattle and was immediately followed by whistles and shouting. Bob Hope quit talking. We had no idea what was going on.

We later learned that a group of women's liberation activists, led by the intellectual Sally Alexander, had not been content to join the protest outside the Albert Hall as we arrived that evening. They bought tickets to the event, dressed up so they looked like they belonged and took their places in the audience. Their intent was to disrupt the pageant and to protest what they believed was the exploitation of women. Alexander said she saw it as an opportunity for a "spectacular consciousness-raising episode" for one hundred million television viewers.

Their plan was to wait until we were all onstage in our bathing suits, at which point one of their number would sound the football rattle and their demonstration would begin. The woman with the rattle got so angry at the sexism of Bob Hope's jokes that she started early. The feminists, scattered high and low throughout the auditorium, jumped up and began throwing paper and flour bombs toward the stage, blowing whistles and waving placards. Others squirted the audience, in black tie and mink coats, with ink-filled water pistols. Stink bombs and smoke bombs were set off, and rotten fruit was thrown. Some braver protesters rushed toward the stage.

Bob Hope stood spellbound before what was happening in the audience. He lowered his microphone and asked a stagehand, "Who are these bastards?" Eventually he decided to be terrified by the challenge, handed the microphone to the stagehand and rushed off to the wings as the cameras rolled. (In fairness, playing the coward had always been a big part of his act.) The same private security guards and policeman who had shielded us outside were now in the hall. They chased the activists, who numbered at least thirty, picked them up and carried them out before any of them could reach the stage. It took several minutes to restore order to the proceedings. None of the contestants felt terribly threatened by anything that had occurred, and some yelled at the police to let the protesters down as they were being carried out.

Julia Morley would later say that she had caught Bob Hope as he made his dash off the stage and held on to his foot to make sure he didn't leave the hall. He was coaxed back out in front of the cameras where apart from one good line—"For a minute there I thought I was back in vaudeville"—he failed to recover his composure.

"Anyone that would try to break up an affair as wonderful as this has got to be on some kind of dope."

He rushed through the remainder of his material and, still getting no laughs, began explaining his jokes. He was discombobulated, visibly angry and unentertaining. It was not a highlight of his career.

We had been ushered back into the dressing room during the commotion and given little information about what was happening, but we were too busy with our costume changes and preparations to give it much thought. When Bob Hope finished, the remaining contestants were to make their appearances in bathing suits. I was confident that my outfit stood apart from the others. Two-piece bathing suits had not been allowed since the very first Miss World contest (which was, in fact, a bikini contest). Mine was a one-piece suit but the transparent material at the sides, separated by a narrow strip of fabric down the centre of my torso, was as close as one could get to a two-piece without violating the rules. The white material was an attractive contrast to my darker skin.

As I walked, Michael Aspel told the audience: "One of the smallest places to be represented in this year's contest, and for the first time, is Grenada, not to be confused with Granada in Spain. From the Caribbean, Grenada's representative, Jennifer Hosten, twenty-two years old with statistics of 36-24-38, is five feet seven inches, with large brown eyes. Jennifer, who is now an air hostess, was formerly an announcer with the BBC's Overseas Service. She is also a qualified secretary. Her hobbies are dancing, yoga and tennis."

It was in the bathing suit event that I first felt the support of the crowd. The cheers and whistles I heard sounded more spontaneous than the applause showered on the girls who had gone before me. Shouts of "Good for you, Jenny!" and "We want Grenada!" from my home-country cheering section were quite audible.

After the last contestant had walked in her swimsuit, we were all invited back onstage as a group and asked to first face the cameras and then turn around, showing our backs to the audience, or "the other point of view," as the announced put it. This was the moment that the feminist activists had originally planned to exploit. It would be years later, when I lived on a farm and visited a sales barn and saw the auctioneer turn the cattle around in the ring, before I understood the allusion to a cattle market. It was not inappropriate, and the Miss World organizers soon dropped this part of the pageant.

After this gathering onstage, we waited for the results of the second elimination. Once more I was chosen, this time as part of the final seven contestants, three of whom were women of colour. Again, the disappointment on the faces of girls who had not been chosen was very evident. Chaperones hastened to pass on good words to lift the spirits of the disappointed girls. One of the most obviously upset contestants was Miss Norway, who sat alone refusing the kindnesses of her persistent chaperone.

Now, still in our swimsuits, the remaining contestants were invited onstage one at a time to be interviewed by Michael Aspel. The important thing was to retain one's composure in the glare of a global audience, show some spontaneity and intelligence, or at very least respond sensibly to the questions asked. Again, this was more difficult than it appeared. Most of the girls were breathless, somewhat giddy and unsure of themselves. Some did not know a lot of English. Miss Brazil told Aspel that she wanted to study modern languages. "A little too late for that, isn't it?" he replied. Miss Sweden came off as intelligent but flinty, without charm.

I had guessed that Aspel, as a broadcaster, would ask me about my broadcasting experience, and I guessed right.

"Well, Miss Grenada," he said. "I see you have been in broadcasting. Would you like to interview me?"

"Why, certainly," I said, and without hesitating reached for his microphone.

"Well, we had better do that when we have some more time," he said, smiling. "What are your ambitions?"

"I should like to go into acting, but if I could incorporate that with a bit of broadcasting, I should be delighted."

Again, I felt the reward of strong applause as I walked offstage.

The seven finalists—Miss England, Miss Israel, Miss Sweden, Miss Africa South, Miss South Africa, Miss Brazil and me—appeared once more onstage as a group and then headed backstage with the cameras still on us as the judges made their final deliberations. The television lights were hot, and we were all anxious.

"Who do you think it is?" asked Miss England, who was standing beside me.

"I think it is you!"

"No," she said. "I have the distinct feeling that it is you. Let's see!"

We were all saying similar things to one another, except for Miss Sweden, the favourite of the oddsmakers, who was convinced that she was going to win. If I had been obliged to bet on the outcome at that moment, I would have said Miss Africa South or Miss Israel, but I had not seen either of them onstage so I did not have a good sense of how they were doing. I was convinced by this point that I had done all I could, and I was saying to myself, "At least I've made it to the finals. I have represented Grenada well, whatever happens." And then came the results, in reverse order.

Miss South Africa placed seventh. Miss Sweden was sixth. She had to have been shocked, but she kept her composure as she walked back onstage to collect her trophy and a cheque for one hundred pounds. Next was Miss Israel, who had gone into the army at a young age yet had a soft, thoughtful manner and was a favourite among the contestants. Then came Miss Africa South, Pearl Jansen, who kissed the rest of us quickly and almost ran out onstage to take her position with the other two behind the throne.

That left Miss England, Miss Brazil and me, standing side by side in front of the cameras, smiling and dying of suspense.

CHAPTER EIGHT

Introducing
Miss World 1970

MERCIFULLY, THERE WAS LITTLE more waiting to be done. I had just noticed the strangest feeling in my stomach when I heard the announcement: "And Miss World 1970 is Miss Grenada!"

I was stunned and, for the first time that evening, unprepared. My first thought was that I must not cry. I felt the tears welling up and wanting to come out, but my pride held the upper hand. I managed to keep my head up and control my emotions. I thanked Miss England and Miss Brazil for their hugs of congratulations, and someone said, "They are expecting you onstage."

I walked out before the audience to thunderous applause, not entirely sure where I should be, but I saw Michael Aspel out of the corner of my eye, and he directed me to the throne. I sat down as two attendants in frock coats, knee britches and periwigs came out to drape the golden cape over my shoulders. A Mecca official handed me the sceptre. Then came Bob Hope with the crown. "Jennifer," he said, "you deserve this. I hope your talents and good luck give you a wonderful year." The crown looked enormous up close and felt heavy on my head. I was scared to death that I would knock it off.

The orchestra struck up the first bars of the Miss World Victory March, a stirring anthem composed, we had been told in rehearsals, by the father of Mrs. Morley. I now walked, as we had all been taught in rehearsals, in time with the music, and I could see Eric Morley walking along the edge of the stage, timing me. I stopped in front of the judges to acknowledge and thank them, and proceeded to three other positions on the stage. Finally, I turned once more in the throne's direction, carefully balancing the crown, which, as I had joked to Pommie earlier in the evening, did seem to sit well on my hair. The music came to an end just as I finished the walk and sat back down. I felt I had managed this sequence with the grace and poise I had intended. One of the reporters credited me with "a quiet dignity rarely seen at beauty contests."

As I sat back on the throne, more photographers than I had ever seen in one place rushed forward and began popping their flash bulbs. For a moment or two, I was struck dumb. Questions were being thrown at me as rapidly as the flashes.

"How do you feel?"

"Will you speak to your folks on the telephone?"

"What is the first thing you'll do in the morning?"

"What do you think of the runners-up?"

"Do you feel like crying?"

One photographer said, "Come on lass, give us a wink, you know, a winning sort of wink."

I complied and the "winning wink" made headlines the next day.

My family gathered backstage to congratulate me. One enthusiastic member of the Grenada contingent wept until her face was quite wet and, consequently, after the hug and kisses, so was mine. I had to fix my makeup before the cameras returned.

Meanwhile, Pearl Jansen, who had come second, said to me,

"Congratulations, you deserve it. Never mind what people will say. They will say that we should not have won, that it is politics that two coloured girls should come in first and second, but just keep your chin up. You deserve it. Remember that!" Long after, I would find comfort in her words.

I was told that I could not stay at the Albert Hall for security reasons and so I was bustled into a waiting limousine and driven to Café de Paris, a Mecca establishment in the West End of London and the venue of the Miss World Ball. It was just as I was leaving the hall that I was told that my evening gown had mysteriously disappeared. I was still in my swimsuit.

Café de Paris was brightly lit, and the long line of cars out front indicated a huge attendance for the ball. A smartly dressed commissionaire opened my car door, and we alighted. My Mecca protector, a stocky man by the name of David, announced, "MISS WORLD 1970." In I walked with my bathing suit on, only slightly hidden by the cape, which fell to my ankles but was open to the front. I was taken along a gallery, and as I looked over the rails into the large room below, I saw a very elegant hall filled with people. Chandeliers hung from the ceiling, and as the band struck up a waltz, ladies in fashionable evening gowns floated across the floor.

I obviously could not make a grand appearance at the ball in my bathing suit. I was told that several assistants were searching for my gown and that until they found it, I would have to wait in a cloakroom, the only private spot in the whole of the Café de Paris. In we went. Pommie and I were introduced to the attendant, an Irish lady with a warm disposition and friendly face. Over the next ninety minutes, we were joined by my sister Aileen and Audrey Palmer, one of Mrs. Protain's party, while other members of my family were awaiting my arrival in the ballroom. At first, we sat and chatted about the results of the contest. As time slipped by, we were glancing more frequently at our watches.

At one o'clock, Pommie asserted herself. "Girls," she said, "we simply have to do something. They can't expect Jen to sit here any longer. It's ridiculous. Think of all the people downstairs. They must think she's been kidnapped or something."

We found a young man employed by Mecca waiting outside the cloakroom and summoned him to find out if there was any news of the missing gown. He came back to tell us they had not found it. Audrey Palmer, the only member of our party with something approximating my measurements, offered to let me wear her dress. It was a princess-line dress made from white jersey, long with a low neckline, and covered with tiny white beads. It fit remarkably well, and quite soon I was ready to make my grand appearance. Poor Audrey put on her coat over her underwear and unselfishly suggested that she continue to wait in the cloakroom until word came of the arrival of my own dress. She said that she felt sure that it would turn up soon.

The Mecca employee escorted me down the steps and suddenly the band stopped playing "Close to You" and struck up "The Most Beautiful Girl in the World." Everyone clapped and cheered, and I was led to a chair at the head of a long table. The card in front of me read "Miss World." The waiters brought a menu, and I was handed champagne. It appeared that I was one of the last people to eat. Before my food was delivered, I was asked to dance by a middle-aged gentleman with sparse hair on his head. I would have refused on the pretext that my dinner was soon to arrive, but the Mecca man gave me a wink that said, "Dance with him, luv, if you know what's good for you."

He turned out to be the head of one of the largest film companies in Britain. He mentioned a part, which he said would be mine if I liked. "I'll have to send the script to Mecca, but I don't think you will have any trouble with it," he said. He stepped on my toes through a set of three waltzes before returning me to my table.

I had a couple of mouthfuls before more interruptions from people wanting to congratulate me and gentlemen wanting to dance. Many of the contestants could be seen dancing with their escorts. They either waved at me or left their partners temporarily to congratulate me. Miss India seemed genuinely pleased at my win, so was Miss Japan. My roommate, Miss Malaysia, had tears in her eyes. Later, she said to me, "You deserve to win, Jennifer, if anyone says anything else, they are just jealous." Miss Sweden was one of the few who offered no congratulations. She did not look me in the eye at the ball.

At about two o'clock, word came that my dress had been found lying in the back of a bus, thrown on the floor with some of my other possessions, presumably by an angry contestant. With a Mecca bodyguard asserting a claim on me, I had to force my way to the cloakroom to put on my dress, returning Audrey's with gratitude. (Audrey was as happy to have her own dress back as I was to find my possessions intact.)

I went back into the clutches of Mecca's bodyguard and escort, who ensured that by the end of the ball I felt twice as tired and harassed as would otherwise have been the case. He was forever pulling me in one direction or the other to meet his friends, many of them other Mecca employees. I learned from one of my supposedly distinguished dancing partners that he was a bouncer in one of the Mecca dance halls.

The ball went on until three in the morning, after which we returned to the hotel. I was still in the same trance I had been in since the moment I heard my name called. I managed to crash in my bedroom at about four, only to be awakened by the loud bell of my alarm clock two hours later. From there, I had one hour and fifteen minutes to prepare for a press conference. In my short hours of sleep, I dreamed all sorts of dreams. I dreamed that I was back home in Grenada, talking with my folks about the contest, but in my dream,

I had not won and felt no regret. I was happy to have been able to represent Grenada and gain experience from my participation.

It was only now that the knowledge of what had happened suddenly dawned on me. I had been chosen as Miss World, the most beautiful girl in the world. Even in my early morning daze, I corrected myself, deciding that I was not the most beautiful face in the world, an impossible determination for anyone to make. What Miss World meant to me was that I had been selected for some combination of qualities, including an attractive physical appearance. Pommie came as usual to help me dress in a brown-and-white pantsuit, but I insisted she go back to bed and rest as Peter Jolly of Mecca was to accompany me.

BBC Television was waiting for me with its cameras. The producers suggested we take a walk in Grosvenor Square, on the other side of the Britannia Hotel. As we walked past the hotel lobby, a group of the hotel employees stopped us, and each planted a kiss on my cheeks. The same group had signed a card and sent it to me the evening before, wishing me luck and saying that I deserved to win because of my friendly manner and courtesy.

"We gave you good luck, didn't we?" asked Yvonne, the spokeswoman of the group.

"Yes," I replied, "your card gave me real courage."

The hairdresser of the Britannia had also been an ardent supporter of mine. He claimed that I had been the only contestant to give my real name when I made an appointment to have my hair done. The other girls had said, "I am Miss Greece, can you do my hair for me?"

Out in the park, I walked with the crown upon my head, strolling and playing with flowers—when a tiny hand found mine. It belonged to a little Vietnamese girl, who, like me, had been strolling the park when she had caught sight of me wearing a crown. She had come to see what this was all about. She was about nine years old and told me that her name was Mariette Steinam. She wore a pair of slacks and a three-quarter-length raincoat. She asked if she could hold my sceptre, and I gave it to her. The cameramen thought this quite amusing and proceeded to interview the little girl. They asked where she lived. It appeared that her home was near to Grosvenor Square and that her father was an employee of ITV, the competitive station, so ITV got a plug on the BBC network.

After the press interviews, I was told by Pommie upon my return to the hotel that the Eastern Caribbean Commission was having a luncheon in my honour. I attended and had the privilege of meeting the premier of Grenada and chatting to him for the first time. He congratulated me on winning and said that I had been a good representative of Grenada. The luncheon became an occasion for much picture taking as many members of the Caribbean Press, the high commissioner and with other dignitaries were present. Pommie sat on one side of me and Mrs. Protain, on the other.

After chatting and shaking hands for some two hours, I began to feel faint. Both Pommie and Mrs. Protain made excuses on my behalf, and they took me to my room. There were telegrams and flowers everywhere, and we had to perform quite a clearance in order to make room on the bed. One cable was from Martin, my hairdresser: "Sincere congratulations. Glad that I could have helped in some small way." Another was from my parents: "Well done. We are very proud. God bless, Mum and Dad." There were countless others. I was also told that people on the Isle of Spice had danced in the streets to steel bands, Carnival style, and that upon my return to Grenada a public holiday would be declared. I was left to sleep uninterrupted until six that evening. I awoke to a nightmare from which I never entirely awoke.

CHAPTER NINE

Rigging, Racism & Rioting

I T HAD BEEN NOTICED by many who watched the Miss World program on television and by many who wrote it about it for the next day's newspapers that I was mixed race or, in their eyes, black. Some, like the *New York Daily News*, took this in stride: "Black is most beautiful, Miss World judges agree." Others, led by *The Sun* newspaper, saw a conspiracy by the black members of the judging panel, led by the prime minister of Grenada. How else could a black girl with twenty-five-to-one odds have walked away with the title? How could Grenada win in its first year in the pageant? Did Mecca hope to open a casino in Grenada?

Mecca explained that Eric Gairy, like several other members of the panel, had been chosen as a judge because he happened to be in town for a Commonwealth meeting. As an explanation, this satisfied no one. The company might also have mentioned that no one complained about Brits on the judging panel in years when contestants from the United Kingdom had won the title. For his troubles, Eric Gairy was assailed by the political opposition back in Grenada, who said that he should never have been a judge and that there should be an inquiry into the pageant result. It was obvious to them that a Grenadian could not possibly be worthy of a world title.

A spokesman for the BBC meanwhile told the press that the network had been bombarded with calls about the Miss World program, many of which pertained either to Mr. Gairy's presence as a judge or the dangerous lowering of the standard for beauty implicit in the triumph of a person of colour. Eric Morley said that he, too, had received many calls at home: "I think the protests we have had are mainly from racialists annoyed because a coloured girl won."

A number of the judges had been interviewed by the press, and it came out that I had not received the most first place votes. Miss Sweden had. But because no contestant had a majority of votes, first and second place votes were combined in the awarding of the title, and I came out on top. The judging procedures had all been established well in advance of the contest. Not all the judges were happy with the outcome. Joan Collins said, "Miss Grenada just wasn't the most beautiful there. She took the crown because most of the male judges fancied her. Her sex appeal bowled them over." I decided to take that as a compliment coming from one of the great sex kittens in the history of British cinema.

Some contestants, too, were interviewed and were also displeased with the result. "It was ridiculous the way the judging was done," said Miss Ireland. "Miss Grenada didn't even have a nice figure. There is something wrong with the system."

Added Miss Norway: "I started laughing the moment they declared the result."

And Miss Switzerland: "It was all political. I have nothing against coloured girls, but how Miss Grenada could win I don't know."

Miss Australia agreed: "The judges didn't know what they were judging. Miss Grenada should never have won."

Even Eric Morley seemed aggrieved, while admitting what all the contestants knew: "I'm supposed to be an expert, and my choice was Miss Guyana."

I remembered Pearl's prediction and her wise advice and tried to take the high road: "Everybody is entitled to their opinion. I don't think I'm too bad to look at." I couldn't help but add, "Some nasty people try to bring racism into everything. But I'm convinced I won fairly." Mecca would eventually win a lawsuit against one of the best-read English papers for a suggestion that the 1970 Miss World contest had been fixed.

When the controversy blew over, a newspaper journalist confided to me that it had not been aimed at me personally, but at Mecca and its unsavoury reputation. Eric Morley was not held in high esteem by the media. He was viewed as sexist and almost a pimp, living off the avails of young pageant entrants. He seemed to take the hint and put Mrs. Morley forward the following year as head of the Miss World operation. She did not fare much better.

The five women at the heart of the women's liberation protest would appear in court in London's Bow Street Court in December, charged with assaulting police officers and engaging in threatening and insulting conduct. They would turn their trial into a platform to promote their views and eventually received small fines for their efforts. The feminists have always said, "It wasn't about messing things up for the women in the competition" and "We had no quarrel with the competitors," but that position was difficult to accept given that they had carried signs reading, "You Poor Cows." They also singled out a comment I had made in response to a question about my romantic life—"I'm looking for the ideal man to marry"—as though it were the sum of my ambitions and evidence that I was backward and oppressed.

Over time, I came to the view that the feminist protests around Miss World 1970 had contributed to my victory. Not in large part but somewhat, because they were insisting that it was all about beauty and only beauty could win. The judges chose someone who had made a deliberate effort to present herself as a person and performed well in every aspect of the contest. It was "the package," as Pommie and I called it.

On the brighter side, less than two days after my election, I began to receive love letters from around the world, and mainly from Scandinavia. A young gentleman from Denmark expressed his desire to meet me anywhere I chose. He complimented me on my "poise and grace" during the contest and said that my light bronze complexion was particularly desirable to him. I decided to be amused by letters of this nature.

I flew to Grenada from London on November 23. I had asked the Morleys for permission to return home for a week or so before returning to England, my base for the year of my reign. They granted the leave but neither of them telephoned to wish me well or say goodbye. Now that the contest was over, the organizers disappeared. I arrived at Heathrow in an off-white suit with a high round neckline, carrying on my right arm the calfskin coat presented to me as a gift by Swears and Wells. The head of the BOAC airline greeted me and offered his congratulations.

With no direct flight to Grenada, we stopped overnight in Barbados, where I was greeted at Seawell Airport as though I had represented that island personally. I think it was during that brief stop that I fully realized the closeness of the people of the Caribbean. I gave a short press conference while my papers were taken through immigrations. Then I was whisked away to the Hilton Hotel, where I was greeted first by a guard of honour composed of the hotel staff and residents of the Bridgetown area, and later by my own friends and relatives from the Land of the Flying Fish. We had no choice but to stay indoors that night. Our luggage had been misplaced by the airline. We were grateful and relieved for the break.

When we stepped on the Avro prop jet the next day, I was excited, thinking ahead to my parents waiting to receive me at the airport. I was looking forward to basking in the sunshine on some of the world's best beaches, surrounded by family and the comforts of life that only the Caribbean could bring. My mother captured the scene at the airport in her diary:

> *Queen's Park was thronged with people. The pavilion was packed to capacity and on the grounds, thousands of school children, Girl Guides and Boy Scouts, and members of other youth organizations were lined up. Representatives of international press, radio and television were much in evidence.*
>
> *The ceremony opened with an address of welcome by Mr. Everett Woodroffe, chairman of the Miss Grenada Committee. Then followed an address by the premier of Grenada, the Honourable E. M. Gairy, who had been a member of the panel of judges at the Miss World contest.*
>
> *Jennifer then spoke to the gathering. She said she was happy to be back in Grenada and thanked the government and people of the state for having given her the opportunity of taking part in the contest. She said that she had so often met people who did not know where Grenada was. They confused the name with the Spanish town, Granada. She assured her listeners that such a mistake was not likely to recur. She went on to say that she would do her best to advertise Grenada wherever her travels might take her.*

The many letters I received from well-wishers around the world were among the most inspiring experiences of my life. I replied to as many as I could in my own hand, but when the job became far too big, I had to employ the services of a part-time secretary to keep up with the flow of mail. Some of the writers were quite observant about my circumstances, and I found their words extraordinarily touching:

Dear Miss Hosten,

Any criticism you might read in the press about the Miss World contest can only be the voice of the minority, and I trust that you will take it all with the natural dignity you showed on the particular night.

I, personally, chose you as the winner, for I thought you scored one hundred percent on the interview, replying with intelligence.

Many of us agree that you will make a marvellous ambassadress, and if you show yourself as non-reacting to any criticism, you will put shame upon those who may voice it.

I see you as a marvellous example-setter, and your lovely smile, intelligent face and natural diplomacy will serve the world well; we need people like you.

(Signed by an English duchess)

Dear Miss World,

Congratulations, a thousand times.

One can see and know that you are too intellectual to be even bothered about all the controversy in the British press over your success. . .

I wish you all the fortune of this beautiful world, from which I am locked out. Hope you return soon and further show your beauty and charm.

(Signed by a female prisoner at Wormwood Scrubs Jail)

My dear Jennifer,

You were very wonderful and really beautiful—you came first by a long way. I noticed as you came out, when your name was called as the winner, that you put your hand up to flick away a surprised tear, perhaps, but most of the winners collapse in the chair, in tears, and have to be comforted all round. You came out like a queen, with poise, good manners and sweetness to acknowledge your great world.

We have an old Victorian saying that "jealousy is the sincerest form of flattery."

There is no such thing as the colour bar. We are all God's people and meant to live in harmony and peace. [. . .]

Yours very sincerely,

(Signed by a British baroness]

Being new to the pageant world, I had no appreciation for how much attention the Miss World contest attracted. Thousands of newspapers around the world covered the results, often on the front page. I was very suddenly a celebrity, and I quickly learned some hard lessons about my new status and how others would try to exploit it. A freelance photographer who was a friend of mine obtained from my parents a photograph of me as a small baby. He asked to borrow it and promptly sold the photograph to the newspapers without my permission or knowledge. Other old photographs were obtained and sold in the same manner (as were stories from people who might have known me, slightly, as a child). There were no compromising shots of me at any time, thankfully, but some were of poor quality and unflattering, apart from being unauthorized. I understood that I would have to be careful about managing photo approvals.

I never did get much time at the beach. The next couple of days proved hectic as I complied with requests for more photographs and appearances. There was an official reception at Grenada's Government House given by the governor general, Her Excellency Dame Hilda Bynoe, and Mister Peter Bynoe. Some seven hundred guests, representing a cross-section of Grenadian society, attended. One of the many press interviews I gave took place at WIBS, where I had worked after leaving school. The staff told me an extraordinary story. The continuity clock, mounted on the wall of the studio to time broadcasts, came to a dead halt right at the moment I was

Jennifer Hosten as a baby: "The biggest, roundest, brownest eyes"

St. George's, Grenada: Capital of the Isle of Spice

The Miss World pageant's massive, challenging, multi-level stage

The gold dress: "My secret weapon"

The morning after:
"She asked if she could
hold my scepter"

My brother Robin,
my mother and father,
and sister Pommie

Miss Africa South (right): "People will say that its politics that two coloured girls should come first and second"

Courtesy of BBC

Courtesy of BBC

Wearing the crown: "It was heavy. I was always afraid it would fall off"

USO Tour with Bob Hope: The crowds were massive.

Performing
with Bob Hope:
"Anything you can
do I can do better"

Women's liberation protesters disrupt the program
in the Royal Albert Hall

The BBC's huge television audience was a magnet for protesters

The Mighty Sparrow wrote a calypso: "Jennifer Hosten was crowned Miss World/What a mag-ni-fee-cent girl!"

It was a year of travel and appearances, all of which required careful preparations

Another destination that excited me enormously was Nigeria

My background as a flight attendant
and broadcaster was useful
on the tour

I travelled with five suitcases for all of my outfits, shoes, and boots

I was appointed by Prime Minister Eric Gairy (tipping his hat), who was overthrown by my old acquaintance Maurice Bishop (with Fidel Castro) in a coup that prompted the American invasion of Grenada (bottom)

The Reunion on BBC Radio 4: (Top, left to right) The compère, Michael Aspel; protester Sally Alexander; the BBC's Christina Captieux and Sue MacGregor; Mecca's Peter Jolly; (bottom, left to right) protester Jo Robinson; Jennifer Hosten; protester Jenny Fortune.
Below, my official 50-cent Grenadian stamp

With Sophia, David Craig, and Beau,
and (below) the talented Gugu Mbatha-Raw

announced as Miss World. It was the first time the clock had stopped since the station opened ten years before.

Finally, after an exhausting and memorable five days at home, I bade farewell to my family and friends. It was time to make a move and return to London via Trinidad. I would not return until after the Bob Hope Christmas tour in Vietnam, just in time for the New Year, and promised to keep in touch by telephone when possible.

My first priority in Trinidad was to visit the head office of BWIA and formally request a twelve-month leave of absence without pay. My request had been anticipated and was granted immediately. In fact, BWIA organized and sponsored a reception for me at the Hilton Hotel in Port of Spain. It was a wonderful evening event at which I was offered the congratulations of both the prime minister and the governor general of Trinidad and Tobago and presented with a beautiful gold pin depicting a Caribbean steel pan (the BWIA insignia).

The only negative incident during my stay in Trinidad, as I recall, was an unfortunate problem with my makeup. A renowned local beautician had offered to do my makeup, applying some of her latest techniques. The subsequent photoshoot was a disaster due to the excessive application of white around my eyes, giving me the appearance of a panda. The developed images looked so strange that none could be used. I applied my own makeup thereafter.

Staying with Pommie and her husband, Fred, in Port of Spain made the short visit all the more memorable. Trinidad had been my base for some time, but I had given up my rental accommodation prior to leaving for the Miss World rehearsals. Fred had sorted out the contract. He had also started work on arranging a Caribbean tour for me when I returned from the Bob Hope Christmas tour. Mecca had its own agenda for me, but it did not include some parts of the world that were important to me, starting with the Caribbean.

I gave my sister a huge hug before leaving Trinidad. Pommie and I had been through so much together in the past few weeks.

"Good luck, girl," she whispered, with tears in her eyes.

CHAPTER TEN

Touring with Bob Hope

THE MISS WORLD TITLE came with a diamond-studded tiara, a cash prize of five thousand pounds and a contract providing a range of opportunities and obligations throughout the year of my term. I would be based in London and Mecca would arrange appearances for me around the world, covering my expenses, and sharing the fees paid by my hosts. My first duty was the Bob Hope Christmas tour.

There was more to Bob Hope than he showed that night at the Miss World pageant. He had begun entertaining troops after the United States entered the Second World War in 1941 and continued through the Korean War, right through to Vietnam. He had a soft spot for the soldiers: "I looked at them, they laughed at me and it was love at first sight."

US military bases in Vietnam were among our destinations in 1970. Also on the tour were the official Christmas Tour band; the talented Les Brown and His Band of Renown; the Swiss actress Ursula Andress, who had starred in the first James Bond movie, *Dr. No*, in 1962; Johnny Bench, the all-star catcher of baseball's

Cincinnati Reds; The Dingaling Sisters and the Golddiggers, two song-and-dance troupes known for their work on *The Dean Martin Show;* the Broadway dancer Lola Falana; and the popular singers Gloria Loring and Bobbi Martin.

It was, I confess, daunting to contemplate travelling and performing alongside such talent and experience. Here I was, Jennifer Hosten from Grenada, without either acting or singing experience, about to embark on a tour hosted by the legendary Bob Hope, one of the most famous names in the history of show business. I would be performing duets and gag routines with this extraordinary human being. I would have to learn to deliver my lines professionally enough to complement Bob's precise comedic timing. And I would have to do this before thousands of American troops. I thanked my stars for broadcasting experience. It would serve me well throughout the year.

Back at the Britannia Hotel on the morning of December 12, having packed several suitcases in preparation for my departure from the US Air Force (USAF) Base in Lakenheath, Suffolk, I heard my telephone ring. It was the bell captain calling to inform me that my transport had arrived. My transportation turned out to be a beautiful white Rolls Royce limousine. As the last of my baggage was loaded into the Rolls, the smartly uniformed chauffeur held the back door open. I climbed in and settled into the soft leather seat. A nice way to start.

I would be spending three days and nights on the Lakenheath base at the special hotel run by the USAF, and used specifically to accommodate visiting personnel and their families. I was greeted there by smart, uniformed airmen, who saluted as I alighted from the car and escorted me into the hotel. As I entered, my eyes caught sight of an enormous and beautiful bouquet of flowers on a table near the window. There was a card attached that filled me with warmth:

Dear Jennifer,

    Welcome to the Bob Hope Christmas tour. I hope you might be able to join me for dinner this evening. I'm looking forward to introducing you to the others. We'll be meeting at the bar before dinner at 6 p.m.

    Best wishes,

    Bob

During the three days at Lakenheath, I met with Bob Hope and the entire Christmas celebrity entourage. We spent long hours going over routines, learning lines and generally getting to know one another. It was great fun. They were all informal and good company. There were no personality clashes, and I also managed to learn my routines, much to my relief.

One of my most vivid memories from Lakenheath was a press photo session, in which I was required to pose with Ursula Andress. I had seen her in films and had imagined her to be reasonably tall. I suppose all movie stars seem larger than life in their work. In fact, she was short and petite. So much so that before she allowed any shots to be taken next to me, she insisted on standing on a box. I liked Ursula, and we got along very well during the tour.

The Bob Hope Christmas tour began in Frankfurt. From there, we flew to Athens for another performance, and then to Crete, where we all boarded a large troop helicopter and headed out into the Aegean Sea, landing on the deck of an incredibly huge ship, the navy aircraft carrier *USS John F. Kennedy.* Home to more than three thousand officers and men, it was the length of three football fields and stood almost twenty stories high. I was given my own cabin, and I found all the personnel on board accommodating and friendly. They seemed to genuinely appreciate our presence, and their reception of our show was great. In fact, we were wonderfully received everywhere we travelled.

A couple of days later, we were on our way to Bangkok. This was the start of the most adventurous and perhaps dangerous part of the tour. From Bangkok, we flew to a different base in Vietnam each morning, gave our performance and returned in the evening. It was an unusual experience, and precautions were required. Hope's schedule was never announced in advance. There had been a close call for the tour in Saigon in 1964, when a car bomb flattened the Brinks Hotel right next to where Hope was quartered. "A funny thing happened to me when I was driving through downtown Saigon to my hotel last night," he said. "We met a hotel going the other way."

Everywhere we went, it was evident that the men and women on these bases were having a severe and difficult time being there and doing their jobs. It added a weight to each performance, but the troops seemed genuinely to enjoy the show and to appreciate Bob Hope's efforts. The circumstances made us all perform with a little more passion and energy.

I would be introduced at each performance and walk onstage in my famous gold gown, waving and blowing kisses to tens of thousands of soldiers, many of them younger than I. Bob and I would then engage in some light banter.

"Well, Jennifer," he would ask, "what do you think of this reception?"

"It's wonderful, but why are they whistling?"

"They're not whistling—that's steam escaping. They just came to a boil."

He was generous enough to give me the punchline once in a while. "By the way," he would say, "it was quite a wild night in London when you were crowned Miss World."

"Yes, that angry women's lib group screaming, throwing things, charging up onto the stage. I thought they were going to crown you."

We would also sing a duet at each performance in Vietnam, the old Irving Berlin number from the musical *Annie Get Your Gun*:

"Anything you can do, I can do better. I can do anything better than you."

"No, you can't!"

"Yes, I can!"

"No, you can't!"

And so on. It was fun to do.

Something unexpected happened in our very first performance in Vietnam. Bob was onstage, doing one of his routines when he introduced me quite suddenly: "I want you to meet the new Miss World 1970, folks. Her name is Jennifer Hosten, and she comes from a very tiny island in the West Indies called Grenada. Has anybody here ever visited this beautiful little island in paradise?"

There was a short pause, and then, suddenly, this little voice piped up somewhere near the back of an audience of seventy thousand: "I'm from Grenada too!"

Scanning the enormous human mass beneath me, I was barely able to make out a solitary dot, frantically waving an arm to attract attention. It filled my heart to see this distant figure, and Bob must have known how I felt because he immediately invited the soldier to meet us backstage after the show.

It was one thing for this man to be invited backstage but quite another for him to find his way there. At the end of the show, he proceeded to climb over seats, row after row, trying to get nearer the stage and ultimately to the backstage area. All he could hear as he climbed his way forward was "Hey, where do you think you're going!" and "You can't go there." He refused to stop and did make it backstage, where he asked to see Jennifer Hosten and was told, "You can't see her. She can't be disturbed."

Still refusing to give up, this soldier finally found a captain to whom he explained that Miss World was from the same tiny island that he called home and that he was an acquaintance and Bob Hope had invited him backstage. "Please help me get a message to her." The captain believed him and relayed the message.

His name was Bill Marryshow, and he went by the curious nickname Smico Bill. He and my brother Robin had been school friends and occasional enemies during their time together at Grenada Boys Secondary School. I remembered one particular fight in which Smico's shirt had torn. He had turned up at my home in Church Street to ask my father to replace the shirt. Smico Bill was quite thrilled, as I was, to meet so far from home. He told me that he had lived for several years in the United States and had been in Vietnam since the start of the war, working as a helicopter mechanic. He was very much looking forward to returning to family and friends in Grenada sometime in the near future.

Bob Hope met and spoke with Smico, and I introduced him to all of the entertainers. He was particularly happy to meet Lola Falana, the singer and dancer, who gave him her autograph. Smico was then invited to a little party after the show where he dined with us all. Meeting Smico in Vietnam was a miracle neither of us would ever forget. Years later, we spontaneously reunited and spoke of how it was a moment of real pride to both of us to find one another so far from home.

One day during our tour, it was suggested that I might like to visit a military hospital in Vietnam. I readily agreed, hoping that such a visit would serve as a morale booster for some of the sick and injured troops. The hospital facilities were basic, at best, with row upon row of beds under large tents. Many of the patients I visited had been badly injured. Some were missing limbs that had been destroyed by land mines. Others had suffered second- and third-degree burns or deep shrapnel wounds. It was a sad and depressing, to say the least, but I was glad to think I could offer them some cheer.

At one point, I proceeded without formality from one sick bay to another and was gently but firmly apprehended by an officer before reaching the entrance to the tent.

"You can't go there, Miss. There are no American servicemen in there."

I looked at the officer curiously. "Oh? Are they prisoners of war?"

"No. It's a sick bay for the Vietnamese."

"Vietnamese? You mean South Vietnamese allies?"

He nodded awkwardly, yes.

"Then why can I not visit with them? They are fighting for the same cause, surely."

"Yes, Miss, that's true. But you're here to entertain US military personnel and not Vietnamese. I'm sorry, but I can't allow you to enter that bay."

I stared at him in absolute disbelief. Not wanting to cause a conflict—I could see it would get me nowhere—I turned abruptly and headed back to the main camp without a word. What an appalling situation it was that these sick and maimed people, directly involved in combat and wounded as a result of fighting alongside American soldiers in a ghastly war, were not considered deserving of some of the comfort we were there to bring.

After the hospital visit, our USAF Boeing 707 returned us safely to Bangkok, then to the grand Erawan Hotel where we were staying. Thailand escaped colonialism but nevertheless showed a strong influence of colonial architecture in some areas. The Erawan's stately features and ambience were similar to those of the Raffles Hotel in Singapore. Within minutes of our arrival at the hotel, we were to learn the awful news that Saigon, from where we had taken off, had been heavily bombed in an attack that began twenty minutes after our departure.

We stayed just one week in Bangkok, getting up at five o'clock to reach the airport by eight, and returning to the hotel at about eight in the evening. From there, we travelled to Alaska, plunging from the tropics into an icy climate at the coldest time of year. I had never ventured so far north. I found it uniquely beautiful and inhabited by warm, hospitable people, but oh so cold. One of the highlights was riding through the streets of Anchorage on a sled pulled by a team of huskies.

I was sad not to share Christmas with my family but looked forward to joining them before long and seeing in the New Year. I felt worse for Ursula on Christmas Day. She was not herself. She had just ended a long-term relationship with the French actor Jean-Paul Belmondo. They had spent several wonderful Christmases together, and she was feeling lonely now: "Jennifer, I know it sounds silly, but I really miss him big time. I wouldn't have joined the tour if we had got back together."

On December 28, our USAF Boeing 707 finally touched down at Los Angeles Airport in California, marking the end of the 1970 Bob Hope Christmas tour. It was considered by all involved to have been a great success. From my point of view, it had been an incredible few weeks and a real honour to be associated with such wonderful people. More than anything, I enjoyed the privilege of singing songs with the legendary Bob Hope, one of the best-known show business personalities of all time and, without doubt, the world's leading entertainer of troops. His material might have been somewhat dated, but he proved himself a true gentleman and, most importantly, a great human being whose kind and thoughtful nature pleased everyone we met along the way.

As we all went through customs and entered the arrivals lounge, it became apparent that there were many more people hanging around than there should normally have been, even for LAX. As it turned out, the media had publicized the return of the Bob Hope Christmas tour, and people had shown up out of curiosity and to get autographs. Dolores Hope had arrived with members of her family to meet her husband. It was a wonderful reunion for them. Bob was so delighted that he put on an impromptu performance for the media and bystanders.

I will always remember one special moment from the Bob Hope tour. It was on one of our daily flights from Bangkok to Vietnam aboard the USAF chopper. I had been watching Bob, for what seemed a long time, writing on cards, placing them into envelopes and addressing them. When I asked what he was doing, he said, "Well, you see, gal, I've met many special people over the years. They will always mean a lot to me even though they might be a long way away. This is my way of telling these people each year that they are never forgotten and that I value their friendship. I hope to keep in touch with you as well after this year, so you can expect to hear from me."

True to his word, I received a New Year's card from Bob and Dolores Hope for years to come. Almost two decades later, in the late 1980s, while I was residing in Ottawa, Canada, I was made aware that Bob was coming to the city to perform in a charity show at the Ottawa Civic Centre to commemorate a national holiday. I sent a note to the hotel where he was staying, letting him know that I was also in Ottawa. I welcomed him to the city and said that I would try to attend the show.

Sitting in the audience that evening, I suddenly heard Bob say, "If Jennifer's in the audience, I'd like her to come down here onto the stage. Jennifer's the gal who came with me to Vietnam back in 1970. Ladies and gentlemen, if she's here tonight, I'd like to introduce you to the gal who thrilled thousands of our troops over there and brought a lot of pleasure to them. Come on down here, Jennifer Hosten, Miss World 1970!"

I was astounded by what I heard and was completely off guard as I stood and proceeded down the long steps to the stage to join Bob under the spotlight.

CHAPTER ELEVEN

Miss World Around the World

W HEN I RETURNED TO London in January 1971, some of my real work as Miss World began. Mecca, as mentioned, owned dance halls, restaurants, nightclubs, bowling alleys, and similar venues all over Britain. I made a tour of them, often in the company of Miss United Kingdom, Yvonne Ormes; Ken Dodd, the buck-toothed comedian who was a regular on UK television and quite famous at the time; and Bruce Forsyth, the actor and game show host (who would later marry a former Miss World).

In this way, we hit Mecca properties in London, Manchester, Liverpool and many other cities, some of them grand facilities, others less so. After being introduced, I would perhaps say a few words and meet local dignitaries or mingle with the patrons of the establishment. I did not mind these appearances, but they required a lot of preparation and organization on my part.

For each event, I would have to decide what to wear and get my hair and makeup ready each time. I was fortunate to find a hairdresser from Grenada named Suzanne Mary Smith. If I had time,

I would go to her salon. If I didn't, she would come by and simply comb my hair and give it a style. There was not always time because the events could be on short notice. It helped that I was an organized person. My time as a flight attendant, where I would often get called on four- or eight-hours' notice, had made me especially methodical about preparations.

The excursions would usually begin with the Rolls Royce pulling up at my hotel and the chauffeur, after helping me into the back seat, driving off to parts unknown. There was no briefing about where I was going or what I was to do, and I was often alone, without a chaperone or anyone to guide me or assist me through whatever place or event I was to attend. I was quite vulnerable to the people I was about to meet (some of whom would be well refreshed), but fortunately I managed to avoid any regrettable incidents.

Over time, I learned how to navigate the Mecca organization and get my schedule in advance. It was a matter of who you knew and which member of the extended Morley family you had to see about particular matters. One of the more memorable destinations in this run was Brighton, the seaside resort town. After making various promotional appearances for Mecca there, I accepted an offer to stay on for a few days with an old friend of mine, a Barbadian fashion designer by the name of Anthony Roach. Anthony and his friend Geoffrey escorted me one evening to a British Conservative Party dinner and dance at the Grand Hotel, where I met and danced with British Prime Minister Edward Heath. I found him to be a quiet, gentle and most interesting man with a great passion for music and the arts.

The following day, I visited the beauty salon at the famous and sumptuous Regency-period Hippodrome Hotel. I had accepted a gift from the hotel of a day's pampered indulgence in their exquisite spa and beauty salon. It was there that I recognized the legendary film actress Ingrid Bergman, star of *Casablanca, Joan of Arc* (for which she won her first Academy Award) and some of Alfred

Hitchcock's best movies, lying next to me and receiving a massage. When my masseuse asked how I felt about being Miss World, Miss Bergman overheard and introduced herself to me. She was so interested in all that had happened at the Royal Albert Hall to the point that she almost made me feel like a star. It was awkward, given her momentous achievements.

Early in the year, I vacated the Britannia Hotel. Since my crowning, I had begun to feel as though I were living in public. Mecca arranged for me to stay in places that were useful to the company, but I took control of the situation, first sharing an apartment with a girl on Baker Street and later, after speaking to my mother by telephone, with a Grenadian friend we called Aunt Ethel. "She has a lovely place, and I'm sure she would love some company," said Mom, and she was right.

I was happily installed in the home of a wonderful Grenadian woman where I could enjoy some home-cooked meals, a true family atmosphere and, when I wanted it, privacy—Aunt Ethel screened my telephone calls. She lived in a quiet, central area near Notting Hill Gate. I stayed with her the rest of the year, and every time I returned from my travels, it felt like I was going home.

When I signed my contract with Mecca just after winning the pageant, I had arranged to do my own tour of the Caribbean, a region of no particular interest to the company but important to me. Fred Thomas, my brother-in-law, was a sharp businessman, and he arranged an island-hopping schedule for me. I began in Trinidad, where I was able to reconnect with so many friends and colleagues from BWIA. We had a fantastic party at the home of Jennifer Selman, a fellow flight attendant, and in true Trinidadian fashion, the dancing went on through most of the night.

In Barbados, St. Lucia, Dominica and Jamaica, I met heads of state and dignitaries, and members of the general public, and felt once more how important my victory was to people throughout the region. I was impressed at how much these islands had in common. What a pity, I thought, that the effort to construct a larger West Indian Federation in the Caribbean had failed in the early 1960s.

Near the end of this tour, I returned to Trinidad for an appearance in the Savannah, a sprawling park in the centre of Port of Spain. It was and is often used as a venue for large events, especially Trinidad's annual carnival. On this occasion, I was joined onstage by the world's greatest calypso artist, Slinger Francisco, better known as The Mighty Sparrow. Born in Grenada, he was a popular recording artist and, along with Harry Belafonte, largely responsible for the embrace of calypso music around the world.

The Mighty Sparrow had written a calypso in my honour called "Cousin Jennifer." He performed it for the first time in public that evening:

> *Jennifer Hosten was crowned Miss World*
> *What a mag-ni-fee-cent girl*
> *With grace and elegance*
> *That is how to charm the audience*
> *Nobody else had a chance*
> *Three cheers for you, cousin Jennifer*
> *The fairest of all*
> *That is what you are*
> *Charm and mannerism*
> *Poise and magnetism*
> *And stepping in style*
> *With a lovely smile*
> *Oh, how we love cousin Jennifer*
> *And we are all very proud of her. . .*

The Caribbean was one of a number of tours that I arranged on my own, rather than under the auspices of Mecca, to take full advantage of my year. I would find gaps in my schedule and ask Julia Morley if she had any problem with me organizing things to fill them. "No," she would say, "as long as it doesn't interfere with your schedule with us." Off I would go to France, where my brother organized some appearances for me.

I was extra cautious in my dealings with the Mecca people to ensure that they did not mind me doing outside events and that they would not expect to share in any appearance fees I received for them. I called Julia to discuss these terms, and I took the precaution of recording the phone call, in case someone else at Mecca might say afterwards that I owed the company money for this or that. The recording was unnecessary, as it turned out, but Mecca, when you saw it close up, was the kind of business that made one careful.

Another destination that excited me enormously, and in which Mecca had no interest, was Nigeria. I had never been to any part of Africa before. Because the country is predominantly Muslim, especially in the north, women were not well treated and in public wore the most conservative attire, including burkas to cover their faces. The city of Lagos, however, was more moderate and progressive, and I was pleased to accept an invitation from Cherry Thompson, a Jamaican woman in England who had helped to organize the visit and served as my official chaperone throughout.

Cherry and I were met at Lagos airport by a local promoter, Mr. Abrahim, and Henry Subair, a nephew of Oba Akenzua II, the sacred king of Benin. Subair was quick to find an opportunity to take us aside and express some concerns about our visit. It turned out that Abrahim had a dubious reputation when it came to ethics and honour. This unfortunately matched our first impressions of Abrahim, who had shifty eyes and a permanent insincere smile. Cherry and I were alarmed and grateful for the warning.

Some of our events went quite well, and the various media representatives and corporate sponsors we encountered could not have been more pleasant. We were taken sightseeing whenever possible. Among the loveliest and most interesting places we saw were the ancient towns of Apapa and Benin, with its sculpted iron artifacts. My only complaint was that nothing in Nigeria happened on time. Traffic was heavy, and people were always late. People complain about Caribbean time, but it is nothing compared to Nigerian time.

We got the full Abrahim experience the morning of our second day. After breakfast, Cherry and I went out to the limousine that was waiting for us in front of our hotel. Abrahim greeted us, that sickly smile pasted on his face. He ran us through the day's schedule, and we set off for the headquarters of Lux Soap, one of our major sponsors. I was surprised to see, as we negotiated the Lagos traffic, an enormous poster of my face advertising Lux Soap. Cherry and I looked at one another and burst out laughing. Abrahim turned around from the front of the limousine and grinned inanely at me.

About fifteen minutes into our journey, the limousine pulled over and stopped. At first, we thought we had arrived at Lux headquarters. When we got out of the car, we found that we were parked outside a large shoe store. It was a confusing moment, and the language barrier did not help. We were pushed toward a small greeting party of men dressed in dark suits at the main entrance to the store. Abrahim introduced me to each man in turn. One was apparently the owner of the store. He invited us in to look at some ladies' shoes. The moment we stepped inside, photographers surrounded me and let loose a frenzy of flashes. To my astonishment, I caught sight of Abrahim in the middle of the crowd of photographers, unashamedly holding out his hand to accept wads of banknotes from them.

Cherry was furious, and once we got back through the door toward the limousine, she blasted Abrahim and demanded an explanation for his behaviour. All she could get in response was a shrug and another sickening smile.

Oba Akenzua II held a ball in my honour at his palatial home
in Lagos. I was invited to take my seat beside him. Seated quietly
on the other side of him, in order of seniority, were his six wives. It
was an unusual and memorable evening. The taste and presentation
of the food were exquisite, and the band was excellent. The oba,
with whom I enjoyed several dances, was charming and very well
educated. Judging from his impeccable English, I thought he had
probably attended Eton or Harrow and Oxford or Cambridge. After
the superb banquet, I found an early opportunity to excuse myself
and circulate for a while. Gloria, a Guyanese girl employed as a
broadcaster at a Lagos television station, came up to me and took
me aside with a look of urgency.

"Jennifer," she said, "I've lived here in Nigeria for several years
now. I know enough, believe me, to warn you. Please be careful.
I think the oba is paying a lot of attention to you, and if he takes too
much of a fancy to you, he may decide to detain you against your
will. He may try to make you his seventh wife!"

It did not know how seriously to take her warning, but it was
sobering. At no time had I flirted with the man. We had simply
danced and chatted. I saw him as my host and enjoyed his company.
I thanked Gloria and for the rest of the night tried my best to keep
my distance without giving any appearance of intentionally avoid-
ing him.

Henry Subair, I learned, was studying medicine in London. His
uncle had assigned him to travel around with us during our tour, and
I could see he was enjoying his responsibilities. In fact, I could tell he
liked me since he took every possible opportunity to be around me.
At one point, Henry asked if I would consider going out with him
when he returned to England. I replied that my schedule was rather
hectic and it would largely depend on when the invitation came. He
smiled and told me he could be very persuasive. Although I liked
him as a friend, I did not want to encourage him too much. I was not

a Muslim, and we appeared to have different values. Besides, I had been dating a Canadian man whom I had first met several months before on one of my flights as a BWIA hostess. I was not seeking to further complicate my life.

We had another Abrahim moment before leaving Lagos. The day before we were to fly out, we received a bill from the hotel management. It was unexpected because the agreement between Cherry and Abrahim was that he, as promoter, was responsible for our accommodation and meals during the tour. We informed the hotel's manager of this fact, and although he believed what we told him, he was clearly concerned that if we did not pay the hotel bill, no one would pay it. No doubt, like everyone else, he knew Abrahim's reputation.

Cherry and I pondered the situation and decided we should call a press conference. Through some Trinidadian contacts, we were able to arrange this for the next morning. I produced a copy of the contract stipulating that Abrahim, as promoter of the tour, undertook to meet all the costs of our visit for both my chaperone and me, including our return air fares to London, hotel accommodation, meal expenses and limousine costs. I thanked the press for their cooperation during my stay and said that we had thoroughly enjoyed our visit to Nigeria, although we were embarrassed and bewildered by some discrepancies concerning our arrangements. I said I hoped that these discrepancies would be resolved as quickly as possible after our departure and that none of the people who had participated in our tour would be uncompensated. We then bade our farewells and headed for the airport, confident that Abrahim would have no choice but to make good on his commitments.

CHAPTER TWELVE

Swept Off My Feet

THE LONGEST OBLIGATION I HAD as Miss World was a springtime tour of Australia and New Zealand, and by the time I was to leave, I did not want to go. I had been travelling non-stop since the previous autumn, and I was feeling tired and lonely, hardly in the mood to journey alone for more than three months on the other side of the world, where I knew nobody. But Mecca had a contract with Joe Brown Enterprises in Dunedin that required the newly elected Miss World to tour New Zealand along with that country's entrant in the pageant. I had no choice. I boarded the plane with a sense of trepidation bordering on panic.

Thankfully, I was allocated a chaperone in New Zealand, a wonderful woman named Daphne Francis. She and her husband, Ron, became and remained good personal friends of mine for years to come. In fact, Daphne became godmother to my daughter Sophia some years later. While I was in New Zealand, Ron suffered a heart attack. Fortunately, he recovered, but Daphne had to leave our tour to devote her attention to him at his bedside in an Auckland hospital. Dennis Brown, a sheep farmer and son of Joe Brown, stood in as my chaperone in the meantime.

The tour was much more fun than expected, and my trepidation soon lifted. I was in the company of a folk group called Hogsnort Rupert Band; the Billy Peters Show Band (a wonderful Maori ensemble); the singer Eddie Low, who had a Roy Orbison–style act; and others. I became instantly attached to New Zealand, its beauty, and most importantly the wonderful people. The Maori I found to be proud, friendly, interesting, caring and blessed with considerable artistic and musical talent. I became close with members of Billy Peters's band as we travelled thousands of miles together on the official tour coach.

My role was to give radio, TV and press interviews to promote the tour and make appearances at our events. It was on one of the long coach trips that I was persuaded to make a recording. Unbeknownst to me, Dave Luther of the Hogsnort Rupert Band was passing some time on the coach by writing a tune for me. One day he tapped me on the soldier from the seat behind mine.

"Jennifer! I've got it."

I was half-asleep at the time. "What have you got, Dave?"

"I've written a real catchy little number for you to record when we get back!"

"What on earth are you talking about, Dave? I'm no singer!"

What I said was true, although I had inherited a good if untrained voice, and as I had shown on the Bob Hope tour, I was confident enough to use it in front of a crowd.

"Let me hear what you've come up with, Dave. Perhaps you could hum it for me."

"Sure, love. It sounds like this."

Dave hummed a sample of the tune he had been writing. It sounded somewhat like a calypso. Although simple, the tune was fun and the beat catchy. I liked it and told him so. I still wasn't sure about making a record, but it did not seem to matter because Dave had no lyrics.

That same day on the coach, an hour or two further along our route, one of the Billy Peters's band members, Charlie, was playing the fool and entertaining the others, as he often did. Laughing at his antics, I instinctively patted him on his shoulder and said, "Charlie, you're a good man!"

"That's it! That's it!" Dave Luther exploded. "I got it! I got it! Listen to this."

Dave proceeded to sing a few lines to the tune he had written. Everybody around, including me, agreed it had potential.

"Charlie Was a Good Man" was born in that moment. By the time we finished the road tour, Dave had the lyrics complete, and the song was ready for a first rehearsal. Within weeks of our return to Dunedin, we were recording not only "Charlie Was a Good Man" in Joe Brown's recording studio but also, for the B side, the beautiful poem "Ode to Grenada," written by my mother. I spoke the words to the poem in the recording studio against a gentle background of instrumental music and natural sounds of waves and sea birds.

Amazingly, "Charlie Was a Good Man" was a huge success, remaining at number one on the New Zealand hit parade for six consecutive weeks. I was thrilled, as were the others involved. (To this day, people come up to me in Grenada and render their own calypso versions of "Charlie.")

We promoted the song all we could. One of the first publicity exercises was an interview with media at the top of Mount Cook, New Zealand's foremost playground for skiers and, these days, snowboarders. On the South Island, the mountain is the highest of a stunningly beautiful range not far from Antarctica. I was to be interviewed and then filmed skiing down from the top of the chairlift. Accompanied by Dennis Brown, we were halfway up the mountain on the lift when he thought to ask about my skiing ability. I informed him that I couldn't say for sure because I'd never tried. I could see the horror on his face.

"What the heck are we going to do, Jennifer? This is an important assignment. You can't slide down the mountain on your backside!"

"Don't worry. I feel quite confident about the whole thing. I have good balance, you know!"

And I carried it off. I did not look like a professional skier, but that was neither important nor expected. My snowplow was perfectly adequate for the occasion, and everyone was delighted. The media photographers wanted additional takes (which I declined—no sense pushing my luck). Dennis was visibly relieved at not having to answer to his father about a disaster on the slopes.

Sales of "Charlie Was a Good Man" continued to grow as we travelled from town to town doing television interviews and selling signed copies of the record at cinema theatres. Before leaving New Zealand, I called at the offices of Sir Keith Holyoake, governor general and former prime minister of New Zealand, and a fine and charismatic gentleman. And I met the greatest New Zealander of all, Sir Edmund Hillary, who in 1953 had become the first person to reach the summit of Mount Everest. He was pleased to know that I had studied his book on Everest as preparation for my Cambridge examination several years earlier.

I found it difficult to tear myself away from New Zealand. I loved everything about it, and I had also met Dennis Brown, who became a friend and confidant. The Canadian man I was dating was a long ways away. I was smitten and considered Dennis, who had his own career as a rancher, a serious prospect, but before I could pursue it further, I had to leave for Australia and the last leg of my tour. The departure from Auckland airport was sad, so to cheer myself up I vowed to return in the not-too-distant future.

Most of the little I knew of Australia came from Rolf Harris, the singer-songwriter who in the early 1960s had enjoyed a top-ten hit in England and America with "Tie Me Kangaroo Down, Sport." His studio had been next to mine during my time with the BBC in London. I was always impressed with his extraordinary cartoons and his wonderful impersonations of native Australian animals. Amusingly, he used to refer to me as "Miss Grenada" long before I had thought of entering a pageant. Rolf came to represent for me a typical Australian, extremely laid back, great company and always ready to make fun in a spirit of camaraderie. (Years later, I would be shocked and disappointed to hear the accusations brought against Rolf Harris and Jimmy Savile, his fellow BBC personality.)

We flew across the Tasman Sea on an Air New Zealand DC-10, and as it made its approach over Sydney, I could see the harbour below, its brilliant blue water dotted with the sails of the many yachts enjoying their sport on one of the world's best-known waterways. The famous Sydney Harbour Bridge stood majestically beside Australia's latest landmark, the Sydney Opera House, only recently opened by Her Majesty Queen Elizabeth.

The main purpose of my visit to Australia was to participate in the Quest of Quests, an annual beauty contest that produced the country's next entrants in the Miss World competition. The sponsors, Waltons (a large chain of department stores), benefited enormously from the publicity. The contestants modelled Waltons spring fashions, as did I. It was a highly successful event which took us to Melbourne, Adelaide, Perth and Brisbane in addition to Sydney.

Australia turned out to be another place where I ran into Grenadians far from home. On one occasion, I was near the end of reciting the poem "Ode to Grenada" when I heard someone sobbing in the audience of several hundred people. Glancing around, I spotted an old school friend of mine, Hilary Otway, dabbing her eyes with a handkerchief. I was astounded to see her right there in front of me. We met later, and I learned that she and her husband, an Australian, worked as missionaries in the outback. It was very special to see her and catch up with news about her family and our schoolmates.

Then one evening in Melbourne, the hotel operator called.

"Miss Hosten, there's a Dr. Mitchell here to see you. May I connect her?"

"Thank you, yes," I replied, wondering who Dr. Mitchell might be.

"Hello, is that you, Jennifer? I don't know if you will remember me. I'm Marguerite Mitchell from Grenada. I live and work here in Melbourne. I heard you were here and thought I would drop in to see you. Is this a good time?"

Of course, I remembered her, a contemporary of my elder sisters, Pommie and Aileen. I met Marguerite in the hotel lobby, where we sat and chatted, and I filled her in on everything my sisters were up to. It struck me how many fellow islanders had left their homes to seek their fortunes in faraway places. Australia was about as far away as one could be.

Melbourne I enjoyed more than Sydney, its competitor for pre-eminence in Australia. Sydney has the beautiful harbour and stunning beaches, but Melbourne is a more cosmopolitan city, with wide streets, interesting architecture, museums and galleries, culture and charm. Perth, too, appealed to me, although it felt more like a large country town than a major city. It is on the far side of the vast and barren desert lands of the Nullarbor Plain, isolated from the rest of Australia. Its closer proximity to Singapore and Indonesia gives it an Asian flavour that I had not noticed elsewhere in the country. During a visit to city hall, Perth's mayor presented me with a key to the city, together with a miniature dustbin, the city's symbol of cleanliness.

I was kept busy all the time in Australia, visiting children's hospitals in nearly every city as well as zoos, department stores and media outlets. At the very end of the trip, while judging the finals of the Quest of Quests, the wonderful Marjorie Colbrooke, who had organized my tour, asked if I would consider participating in a show at the Sydney Opera House with the already legendary American pianist Liberace. I was invited to mime (not sing) my own recording of "Charlie Was a Good Man." How could I possibly turn down an opportunity to meet this extraordinary showman, not to mention promote my record? The evening at the Sydney Opera House went smoothly, and I got on well with the gracious Liberace and admired his elaborate costume and large rings. It was a wonderful way to end my memorable Australasian tour in the summer of 1971.

CHAPTER THIRTEEN

New York, New York

I DID KEEP MY PROMISE to return to New Zealand, stopping in Auckland on way back to London. One of the reasons for doing so was to see the gentleman with whom I was smitten. I arrived at the airport. Daphne was there to meet me, along with her husband, Ron, healing heart and all. No Dennis.

"Where is he?" I asked. He had known I was coming.

"He's shearing sheep in the South Island, but he'll come the next day or the day after."

And that was it for me. I decided right there he was not the one. It may sound like a small thing, but his failure to meet me was important to me. I have always been like that. The small things often help me decide at times what is truly important to me. I had a nice time with Daphne and Ron and returned to London where, I must admit, it felt anticlimactic to find myself back in the rat race after such an enjoyable journey. I could have taken up residence in New Zealand but for its remoteness from the world that I knew.

One of the things that had changed for me in London, and not for the better, was my sense of privacy in my little nest at Aunt Ethel's house in west London. The British press had discovered my whereabouts and were starting to hound me. There were only weeks

remaining before the Miss World crown would be handed over to a
new girl, and the reporters had questions:

"What do you plan for the future?"

"Where will you live?"

"Is there a man in your life?"

"Will you get married and have children?"

In fact, on my return to London, I became more serious about
the Canadian I had been dating, David Craig. We had seen each
other a few times in the course of my very busy year—he had sent
me flowers the night I won the pageant—but I was not ready to
announce anything to the press.

It was almost a relief to pack again my five or six suitcases with all
of my outfits, shoes and boots to match, and fly across the Atlantic
to New York, the last major journey of my year. It was my second
visit to Manhattan as Miss World. The first had been in the spring,
and was much more eventful.

On that earlier occasion, I had been met at John F. Kennedy
Airport by representatives of the Grenadian embassy and Burt
Champion, who had been arranged as my New York agent by
Gertrude Protain on behalf of the Grenada Board of Tourism. My
first duty was to appear as a guest on *The Tonight Show* with Johnny
Carson. The following day I was to have lunch with the actress Joan
Crawford at her apartment, a date arranged by Burt.

Our first stops were Bloomingdale's and Saks Fifth Avenue to get
fitted for some of my appearances. During this shopping spree, Burt
encouraged me to visit the hat section at Bloomingdale's.

"Miss Crawford simply loves hats!" he said. "A beautiful hat
would impress her immediately."

I tried on several. Five of them suited me well. It was such a difficult choice that I decided to take them all.

The Johnny Carson show was televised live that night. At about
eight o'clock, I arrived at the studio and met Johnny and his sidekick,

Ed McMahon. We all chatted for a while, during which I was given a synopsis of the show. Ed then invited me to join him for an early dinner at "a nearby restaurant."

The nearby restaurant turned out to be the posh Empire Room at the Walforf Astoria Hotel. The entertainment that night was very special: the one and only Ella Fitzgerald was at the start of an engagement at the hotel. Ella was at her absolute peak, and she performed brilliantly before an appreciative audience. At the end of one of her numbers, she waited for the applause to die and announced that she had a surprise for everybody: "Ladies and gentlemen, I want you to put your hands together and welcome my very good friend and yours, Mister Louis Armstrong!"

I was absolutely amazed. There I was, at one of the best tables in this beautiful restaurant, witnessing a performance by one of the most famous duos in the history of music. It was magnificent but all too short. Ed looked at his watch and turned to me. "Jennifer, I'm afraid we need to be going. The show starts soon." With my head in a whirl, we got up from the table and made our way out.

We arrived at the television studios just in time. Johnny Carson was the most relaxed TV host I've ever met. He was thoroughly professional. His research was all up to date, and he made me feel quite at ease at all times. We spoke about the Bob Hope Christmas tour, my experiences in other countries, and so on. Both Johnny Carson and Ed McMahon were perfect gentlemen. They worked brilliantly as a team and it was fascinating to me to watch the intricate workings of a live show of the highest quality, expertly delivered.

The following day I had to prepare for my luncheon with Joan Crawford. Needless to say, I was thrilled to meet her. She had started her career as a Broadway chorus girl and became one of the biggest stars in the history of Hollywood, winning an Academy Award as best actress for her work in *Mildred Pierce*. She was no longer acting as much as she had in the past—she was probably in her early seventies (her birth date has always been a mystery)—but she was still a star among stars.

Selecting one of my beautiful new hats, I dressed in an elegant new outfit and met with Burt Champion in the foyer of my hotel, from where we took a limousine to the New York apartment of Joan Crawford. She was then living at the Imperial House on the Upper East Side. A well-groomed maid answered the door and escorted us to a spacious drawing room. Joan Crawford obviously loved small dogs. There were at least five of them to be seen, all in good condition and well behaved. Soon Miss Crawford appeared, greeting Burt warmly and shaking my hand. Evidently, she and Burt knew each other well.

At lunch, she asked questions about my experiences as Miss World. We chatted on various other subjects before she asked if I had given thought to becoming an actress. I told her it had crossed my mind.

"I'm a director of an acting school that I founded, Jennifer. If you were really interested, I would be glad to arrange for you to be enrolled on a scholarship."

"But," she went on, "when you get through with acting school, you will no longer be a Miss World. What's more, acting is a very tough business, and there is no guarantee that you would succeed. There are very many people who go through all the training provided, get themselves signed up with good agents, and at the end of the day don't quite make it. That's the reality of the game."

I thought about the stars on the Bob Hope tour, some of whom would not burn for long, and realized how right she was. It was a tough business. I thanked Miss Crawford for her hospitality and her kind offer to assist me in pursuing an acting career. I promised I would give it serious consideration. (I did, and I decided against it.)

By the time of my second trip to New York, I was looking ahead to returning to the Albert Hall and giving up my crown at the 1971

Miss World pageant. I recalled that on the evening I had won, the producers of the show had asked my predecessor, Eva Rueber-Staier of Austria, to perform a little dance routine in front of a global television audience. If I was going to receive a similar request, I was going to be prepared. I would have my own dance routine ready to go.

I contacted an extremely talented Trinidadian dancer living in New York, Geoffrey Holder, who later performed in the 1973 James Bond film *Live and Let Die*. I asked if he might teach me some good modern dance moves that I could use on the occasion. Due to heavy commitments, Geoffrey was unable to help, but he put me in touch with a Norwegian dancer named Avin Harrem. I met with Avin for several sessions at a New York dance hall and learned enough steps to feel ready for the handing-over ceremonies at the Albert Hall the following month.

Miss World 1971 was held on November 10, with fifty-six contestants from around the world. The hair was a little bigger that year and the protests smaller, but little else had changed. Miss United Kingdom was the heavy favourite. She was upset by twenty-two-year-old Lúcia Petterle, a medical student representing Brazil. I had the honour of handing my crown over to Lúcia. I was never asked to perform a dance number, but I had a more enjoyable time for being prepared.

It was a lovely event, and it brought back many wonderful memories of my big night a year earlier. Nevertheless, I can honestly say I was relieved to hand over my title. Miss World had been a great honour, and a real job. For twelve months, I had felt myself under intense scrutiny. Everywhere I went, people were sizing me up. I felt a duty to appear perfect. I had once been sitting in the first-class compartment of a BOAC flight when a gentleman said, "How do I tell Miss World her eyelash is coming off?" As I was fixing it in the washroom, I wondered what my life had become. As I said, frankly, to a newspaper reporter at the end of my term: "It is like living ten years within one . . . It isn't easy at all. The time was very largely spent in making impromptu speeches, modelling, opening functions of every sort. There is a bit of glamour and also a bit of pathos."

I was satisfied that I had represented the title well, and I was eager to withdraw from the limelight and rejoin the real world. At that point, I had no reason to expect that different and in some ways greater adventures awaited me, but I was determined not to spend the rest of my life as a former Miss World. I gave Miss Brazil a friendly kiss on both cheeks, offered her my sincerest wishes for success in the forthcoming year, then joined my sister and friends. We had a great time at the ball.

CHAPTER FOURTEEN

A Grenadian
in the Snow

I HAD MET DAVID CRAIG, a Canadian computer engineer, on a flight back while I was working for BWIA. I was working in first class. He was sitting in economy. Every time I passed, he would say, "Why don't you bring a drink for me?"

"Well, because I'm working up there, but I'll ask somebody to bring it to you."

"No, no, I want you to bring it."

Finally, as the plane was landing, he said to me, "Can I take you out sometime?"

I told him I had a boyfriend—I was going out with a guy from Trinidad—but thanked him very much. That very night, I was standing on the curb outside the airport, waiting for the car to take me home, and the car did not come. I called the dispatcher to ask where it was. The dispatcher said he had no idea. Just then, David Craig drove past: "Going my way?"

"Well, that depends where you live."

It turned out that he lived on the island, a block away from me. He was well dressed and looked like a decent person, so I took down his licence plate number, called the dispatcher and gave it to him and told him not to bother with the car. David dropped me at home, not before asking me out again, and receiving the same answer.

I must have given him my number because he kept calling me and inviting me out. Eventually I broke up with the Trinidadian, and David invited me to a party. He was leaving Trinidad for Bermuda and another job with his employer, IBM. It was his farewell party. I said I would go and then utterly forgot about it. Afterwards, a couple of flight attendants who had gone said to me, "You never showed up at the party."

"What party?"

"David Craig's. He was looking for you the whole time."

Still, he kept in touch. He was always calling. My mother was visiting me in Trinidad once, and the phone rang and I told her, "If it's that Canadian guy, I'm not here." She remembered that so distinctly that when I later got engaged, she laughed, "Not to that Canadian guy that you were never there for!"

The flip side of David's persistence was that he was reliable. If he said he was going to call, he called right on time. If he said he was going to be somewhere, he was there. That mattered to me. Eventually, we went out a few times. He liked to cook and so he would invite me to his apartment and make dinner. He was a very good cook. He would have everything just so. As a matter of fact, he taught me to cook because I'd never learned. (He also taught me to wash clothes and other basic things about which I had no idea.)

Some months later, when I was in London, David was going to South Africa with his father and asked if they could both meet me during their stopover. Before long, he was one of the most stable things in my life at a time of real instability. He popped the question the moment I was no longer Miss World. I said yes.

All of which is a long explanation for how I arrived in Canada in late January 1973. The road trip from Toronto to Ottawa was nerve-racking and unpleasant. We drove 450 kilometres (280 miles) in a winter storm so severe that there were actual snowdrifts on parts of the highway. I don't mind saying I was frightened.

David was driving the car. Our first two years of married life had been in beautiful Bermuda, where he worked for IBM. I liked Bermuda very much, but David was a Canadian who had grown up on a farm and had always wanted to have a large piece of land with a house, which would have been very difficult to organize in Bermuda since we were both foreigners there.

At first, I did not relish the idea of moving to Canada. I remembered the long, cold, daunting winters in Montreal. I nevertheless agreed to give it a try for at least one year, after which we would assess the situation.

About an hour out of Ottawa, the nation's capital, the car in front of us skidded off the highway and landed upside down in a ditch. We stopped on the side of the road and went over to see if we could offer any assistance. The snow continued with driving force. As we approached the upside-down car, a woman climbed through the window. I could not believe her first words: "Is my hair messed up?"

We offered the woman a drive to Ottawa. She was going to Manotick, a short distance from our destination. Talking with her in the car, we learned that her name was Merle Blundie. She was on her way to visit her brother, Jervis Black, a United Church Minister in Manotick.

The snowstorm was still in full force when we arrived at Blue Bird Farm, owned by David's father, Jack, and his wife, Doris. We invited Merle to spend the night, and she gladly accepted. The next morning, her brother and his family came to collect her from the farm. She'd already had coffee and breakfast with us. Country people looked after one another.

News of the arrival of a former Miss World to Osgoode, a small rural community just south of Ottawa, spread quickly. An article appeared in the *Manotick Messenger*, the local newspaper. Our engagement had been followed closely by the *Ottawa Citizen*, in which David's mother was quoted as finding me "very kind and very gentle."

We lived on Blue Bird Farm for the next three months while we looked for a suitable place of our own. The farm was stocked with Holstein cows. The daily milking took place in the early morning at about six thirty and again at about five in the evening. The first time I tried to milk a cow, I was hopeless, and everyone had a good laugh. I soon learned the art of extracting milk by squeezing and pulling down on the teats alternately in a rhythmical routine, allowing the froth to build up in the bucket wedged firmly between my knees. It was an almost hypnotic experience until, occasionally, the cow would become restless and move away.

One morning, my father-in-law asked me if I wanted to come to see a cow freshen.

"Why would you want me to see that?" I replied, thinking the term referred to the mating of cows. He explained that it was birthing.

"This can be a pretty great experience," he said.

I soon saw what he meant. The cow in question was having twins. The first one came out without much trouble, but the second one stuck in the cow's womb. A rope was tied to this second calf's feet, and it was pulled out, a feat of considerable strength. It was, indeed, a pretty great experience. I had only seen something like this before when I witnessed the birth of a lamb in New Zealand.

During my three-month stay on the farm, my parents-in-law had to go away for a few days. They asked if I would look after the meals and the household in their absence. This meant the preparation of breakfast, lunch and dinner for four people: David, his brother who ran the farm, the hired man and me. Meals were fairly basic. Breakfast consisted of eggs, bacon and lots of toast. Lunch included soup and sandwiches, followed by coffee, and dinner involved meat, potatoes and vegetables, followed by pie and coffee. The two farm workers ate heartily. In this manner, I was introduced to such Canadian delicacies as burbot (which looks like a catfish) and Canada geese.

I often accompanied the men when they went fishing. Most frequently, they caught pike or muskie. I also attended a hunter's safety course and bought my own shotgun. This allowed me to go duck hunting in season with the others and shoot the occasional duck.

My first job in Canada was with the Ottawa Travel Agency. I had applied for a position that had been advertised in the local newspaper and was invited to an interview. Some high-powered Ottawa personalities owned the agency, including Lowell Green, a well-known radio talk show personality, and Earl Montagano, owner of the Ottawa 67's, a junior hockey team in Ottawa. On the day of the interview, I was ushered into a room with six men seated around an oblong table. Introducing myself to the board, I waited for the interview process to begin and responded to questions asked about my background in the airline industry. I was offered employment with Ottawa Travel as a salesperson on a commission-only basis.

I rose from the table with a polite smile. "Gentlemen, I don't wish to waste any more of your time. Let me explain my situation. I have financial commitments. I am not, therefore, interested in working in any capacity without a proper retainer."

This said, I went around the table and offered my hand with thanks to each of the stunned interviewers.

Arriving home about an hour later, there was a message awaiting me to call Ottawa Travel.

"Mrs. Craig, the board has reconsidered the offer made to you this afternoon. We have decided to offer you a retainer as requested and hope you will accept. Could you possibly come in and meet with us again tomorrow to discuss the new terms?"

I worked with Ottawa Travel for about six months. I enjoyed the work and got along well with my colleagues. In the meantime, however, I received a letter from Air Canada inviting me to an interview. (I had applied to Air Canada before accepting employment with Ottawa Travel.) My interview was successful, and I decided to take the job: it came with air travel benefits, and after some time, I was able to work out of the Ottawa airport, which was much more convenient for me than the city.

During my time with Air Canada, I was blessed with the arrival of my two beautiful children. Sophia Marissa was born on November 24, 1975, and Beau David on March 18, 1977. On each occasion, I took a maternity leave of three months.

My life in those days, looking back at it now, seems almost surreal to me. I was getting up to go to work at four thirty, since my shifts began at six. I made a practice of parking the car every night at the bottom of our long lane in case of an overnight snowstorm (the road would be cleared but not our lane). First thing in the morning, in the pitch dark and sub-zero cold, I would take a snowmobile to the end of the lane, transfer into the car and leave the snowmobile in its place to await my return from the airport. I would arrive at the office dressed in a snowsuit and snow boots, with my uniform beneath.

David Craig was industrious, to say the least. In spite of the fact that he had a well-paid job as a computer engineer, he had other home-based interests. One of those was a property maintenance contract with two local cemeteries. One day when David was away hunting, his favourite pastime, I received a telephone call from the wife of the United Church Minister in Kemptville. Introducing herself, she explained that they had an urgent need to fill a grave where there had just been a funeral service. I told her that my husband was absent for a few days but, not wanting to let the side down, I would see what I could arrange and get back to her immediately.

My children, Sophia and Beau, were young at the time. Sophia was five years old but much wiser than her years. She was sitting next to me, and upon hanging up the telephone, I instinctively turned to her and explained the problem at the cemetery.

"What do you think I should do, Soph?"

"Why don't you call Paul Mussell, Mom?" came her immediate reply. Paul was a young farmer living nearby, always willing to help out.

"Why, thank you, Soph. That's a brilliant idea!"

I picked up the telephone once more.

"Find a shovel, Jenny. I'll be over with my truck in about half an hour."

True to his word, Paul turned up on time, with a spade and shovel in the back of his small truck. Leaving the two children in the care of my mother-in-law, I went out to greet him, putting my own shovel in the back of the vehicle and jumping in next to him. On the way to Kemptville, we stopped to pick up an old Irishman by the name of Ernie Knox, who had agreed to help us with our mission. Within half an hour, the three of us were hard at work filling in the grave. In the middle of the job, the minister's wife came up to greet us. She was shocked to see me working with the men.

"Mrs. Craig," she said, "I did not intend for you to do this job. Please don't!"

"Oh, that's alright. Don't worry, it's just a job that needs doing. We'll soon be finished."

Another incident that left a lasting impression on me occurred a few years later. Again, my husband was off on one of his hunting trips. It was a bitterly cold and blustery day in deer season, so probably November. The outside temperature was around -20 degrees Celsius (-4 degrees Fahrenheit). I was in the farmhouse with a delightful Danish woman called Mila, who came around each week to help with the housework. At about five in the afternoon, it had become quite dark. The wind was howling, and freezing rain was blowing almost sideways. I told Mila that I was concerned about the animals in the barn. Some of the windows had been smashed in the building, and the poor animals were exposed to the cruel elements. I asked Mila if she would accompany me to the barn to check things out.

Mila readily agreed. We clad ourselves in gloves, coats and boots and set off toward the barn, some three hundred feet from the house. As we approached, we could hear the grunts and squeals of the large pigs housed there. They must have been extremely uncomfortable in the bitter cold. We headed back to the house and returned to the barn with a roll of thick plastic sheeting, a knife and a staple gun. The two of us set to work stapling the plastic over the broken window panes. It was not a perfect job, but it afforded some protection for the animals. When we had finished our mission, we fed the pigs. We broke the ice on the surface of the water pails to allow the animals to drink. Finally, returning to the warmth of the house, I made some hot coffee for the two of us. Mila was a good friend and confidante, and I was becoming a capable Canadian.

CHAPTER FIFTEEN

Her Excellency, High Commissioner

I WAS ENJOYING A RARE MOMENT of relaxation with some magazines one morning in the spring of 1978 when the telephone rang. I answered a call from Grenada.

"May I please speak with Mrs. Hosten-Craig?"

The voice was completely familiar and unmistakable. Sir Eric Gairy, the prime minister of Grenada.

I identified myself and said, "How are you, Sir Eric?"

"I'm fine, thank you. More important, how are you and your dear family?"

"We are all doing just fine, thank you."

"That's splendid. Well, the reason I'm calling you is to ask if you would consider taking on the position of Grenada's ambassador to the United Nations in New York. We have a current vacancy. I think it would suit you well. I would particularly like to have a capable Grenadian woman in the job, and I believe you would be ideal. It would, of course, require that you live in New York."

My head spun with excitement. I nearly had to pinch myself. Taking a deep breath, I responded carefully.

"I am indeed honoured that you thought of me, Sir Eric. I am, of course, most interested in the offer. However, I will need to discuss this with my husband and get back to you. May I call you back in about two days?"

"No problem at all, Jennifer. I understand that such a decision would require a great deal of thought. But I will need to hear from you soon. Two days will be fine. I look forward to hearing from you then. It's good talking to you again. Goodbye for now."

I hung up the telephone slowly and stared at it for a full two minutes before picking it up again and dialling David's number at work.

"David. Could we meet in town and have dinner somewhere tonight? I've just had a call from Sir Eric Gairy in Grenada. He has made me a very interesting job offer which, I think we should discuss alone."

Our children were still young. David had work commitments. There were certain negative issues as well as positive ones to consider. When we met for dinner that night, David was not at all flexible. He was totally opposed to the idea of moving to New York. I had feared as much, and while disappointed, I did not want to do anything to destabilize our marriage and our family. Two days later, I telephoned Sir Eric Gairy. I told him that while we deeply appreciated the offer, I had no choice but to decline since we would not be able to live in New York for personal and family reasons. He sounded genuinely disappointed but assured me he understood my position.

"Jennifer, does that also rule out a similar position somewhere else?"

"Well, I'd certainly like to help if I possibly can. Please let me know if there is something I might be able to take on in a more conducive environment, which would not be quite so disruptive to my children."

Approximately three months later, I received another call from Sir Eric Gairy.

"Hello, Jennifer. Something urgent has come up, which, in light of our last conversation, might be of interest to you. I would like to offer you the position of Grenada's high commissioner to Canada, based, of course, in your own city of Ottawa. I would be most pleased if you could help us out."

The person who was supposed to be accredited as Grenada's high commissioner to Canada, a Mr. Dolland, had decided not to accept the position. Sir Eric asked me if I held Canadian citizenship. I told him I held both Grenadian and Canadian nationalities.

Canadian citizenship had been very easy for me. I had received a phone call one day from the citizenship office asking me if I was interested. The press coverage accompanying my arrival in the nation's capital must have marked me as a potential candidate. The office made the application procedures quite uncomplicated, and in 1975, I became a Canadian.

Ironically, under these particular circumstances introduced by Prime Minister Gairy, my Canadian citizenship proved to be an obstacle. It was not common for a person holding down a diplomatic position in a country to be a citizen of that country. Diplomats have what is known as diplomatic immunity, a form of legal immunity that exempts them from prosecution under the host country's laws. Countries are more amenable to exempting foreign visitors from their laws than they are their own citizens. Sir Eric assured me he would speak with his friend Pierre Trudeau, Canada's prime minister at that time, to seek his assistance in the matter.

Several days passed without my hearing anything further. I went about my daily routine with Air Canada and at home with the kids, not mentioning the appointment offer to anyone except David and his father. Jack Craig was very supportive of my being appointed Grenada's high commissioner to Canada. If I did not take this prestigious position, he said, I would probably spend the rest of my life with regrets. David, going along with his father, was

also more amenable to this idea than he had been to the previous
offer.

I was soon advised that the government of Canada had broken
with tradition and agreed to make an exception in my case. I would
be a Grenadian during the day, granted diplomatic immunity for all
of my job-related duties, and as soon as I arrived home after work
each day, I would carry the status of any other Canadian citizen.

One of my very first duties was to locate a suitable residence
in downtown Ottawa. The previous high commissioner, George
Griffith, had given up his Ottawa residence when he transferred to
New York to take up the post that I had declined. We settled on an
elegant old house in Monkland Avenue, close to the lovely Rideau
Canal that flows through the city—in winters, it becomes the world's
longest skating rink.

I knew that with additional duties to perform, I would need
adequate help with the children. My sister Pommie was her usual
helpful self, arranging for one of my cousins, Annette, who lived in
Barbados, to come to Ottawa, along with one of Pommie's own staff
members, Lenore, who had been personally trained by my sister to
both cook for her family and look after the children. This arrange-
ment worked well for most of my three years in office.

The office of Grenada's High Commission was situated on
Queen Elizabeth Driveway, also near the Rideau Canal and close to
our new residence. The staff at the time consisted of three members,
the first secretary, George Soltysik, and two secretaries. It took me a
long time to get used to being addressed by them as Your Excellency.

Sir Eric had specifically requested that I attend the upcoming
Commonwealth Games in Edmonton as Grenada's unofficial representative (it took some weeks for me to be officially installed). Given
that the office staff had all been in their jobs for at least three years
and knew them well, I had no qualms about leaving them to their
own devices and flew to Edmonton, Canada's northernmost city.

It was June. The air was fresh, and the sky a brilliant blue, typical of the Canadian prairies. I joined members of the Caribbean Corps and other Commonwealth diplomatic representatives from around the globe for the opening ceremonies. Before the parade, I requested an opportunity to meet the Grenadian team, which consisted of two men and two women. I immediately realized that none of these young athletes had proper footwear. When questioned, they advised me that they were wearing all they had.

I was shocked to hear this, wondering how on earth such a situation could have come about. Without wanting to make an issue of it, I decide then and there to fit them out with proper sporting shoes from my own purse and make an official report after the games. The young people were delighted. Their training was no better than their footwear, and they made an average showing at the games, but the important thing was that they represented Grenada well.

Returning to Ottawa, I made the usual round of courtesy calls to my new colleagues, the representatives of other countries ranging from powerhouses like the United States and United Kingdom to others, such as Mali and Barbados, closer in size and influence to Grenada. Before setting off to each appointment, my driver would attach the Grenadian flag to the car's flagstaff, signifying that we were on official business.

News of my appointment preceded me. Reporters from the *Ottawa Citizen* had arrived at our farmhouse in Osgoode to take pictures of my family. The children were young and cute, and the article appeared to be a popular one. I was later given a framed plaque stating that this particular edition of the *Citizen* sold a record number of copies.

Maclean's magazine, a national newsweekly in the style of *Time* magazine, also ran an article on me, and this one led to controversy. The editors of *Maclean's* decided to sensationalize the article by publishing a photograph of me from the Miss World archives.

I was wearing a swimsuit. The choice of photograph no doubt helped with their sales, but much criticism was raised by those who regarded the portrayal as sexist and disrespectful to the office of ambassador. In any event, I was relieved that the story had put their credibility and reputations in jeopardy, not mine. I did not and would not pose for pictures in my new circumstances, and I was never criticized for this policy.

One of the rites of passage for diplomatic people arriving in Ottawa is a trip to the Canadian Arctic. I had heard a great deal about this from other diplomats and very much wanted to go and experience it for myself. When the Department of External Affairs announced a trip the following April, I sent a note to Michael Doyle, chief of protocol, expressing my interest. When I ran into Michael at an official function a week later, I asked if he had received my note.

"Jennifer, I would like to be able to confirm your place with the group, but as I understand it, there are no suitable facilities for women on the tour. In fact. it has come to my attention that no woman has ever gone on the tour for this reason."

I expressed my regret to Michael, saying how much I had hoped to be included but accepted his explanation. Two days later, I ran into Prime Minister Trudeau at another function. I slowly made my way to where he was standing.

"Hello Jennifer," he smiled at me. "How are you getting along, and how are things in Grenada?"

We chatted for a while, and he said, "I understand you're going to the Arctic this year."

"Well, I was very much hoping to go, but I understand there are no suitable facilities for women. I'm disappointed, but I suppose I have no choice."

Trudeau looked at me intently. "You're not going to let that stand in your way, are you?"

"What do you think?"

"Well, I really wouldn't if I were you."

At that moment, others interrupted us, and the matter went no further. The next day, however, I was surprised and overjoyed to receive a telephone call from the protocol department confirming my place in the forthcoming Arctic tour. I had no doubt that Trudeau had interceded. We departed in June from the air force base at Ottawa's airport, about twelve of us aboard a special Canadian Forces Hercules.

My first experience of the Arctic was Iqaluit (then called Frobisher Bay), some twenty-one hundred kilometres (thirteen hundred miles) due north of Ottawa on Baffin Island. That you can fly so far north in Canada and still only be about halfway to the northernmost extent of its landmass gives you a sense of the country's enormous size (as does the fact that you could fit almost thirty thousand Grenadas in Canada).

Frobisher Bay has a tundra climate, with average lows in deepest winter of -32 degrees Celsius (-26 degrees Fahrenheit). The average temperature in June varies between 6 degrees Celsius (43 degrees Fahrenheit) during the day and -10 degrees Celsius (14 degrees Fahrenheit) at night, too cold to permit the growth of trees. The permafrost does not allow taproots deeper than six inches, which discourages the growth of anything tall. It occurred to me that if there was a part of the world with a climate opposite to Grenada's, this was it. It was a strange sensation to play baseball with my colleagues until after midnight, taking advantage of the almost twenty-four hours of daylight during summer in the far north.

We flew west over thirty-three hundred kilometres (two thousand miles) of tundra to Dawson City, which almost a century before we visited had been the headquarters of the famous Klondike Gold Rush. Poets dressed in period garb read us Robert Service's famous poems of the north, and in Whitehorse, the capital of the Yukon Territories, I tried my hand at panning for gold (landing a small nugget). I met a number of Inuit people, some of whom remained my friends for many years, including Edith Josie, an elderly, almost toothless journalist from Old Crow, who told me amazing stories of her life and work. Our Arctic trip was all too short, but I cherish the memory of it.

As high commissioner for Grenada, I was determined to show the cultural side of the Caribbean to Canadians. I was instrumental in organizing a Grenada Night at the Ottawa Press Club. We served all sorts of Grenadian delights, including callaloo, a large leaf vegetable very like spinach; various fish and chicken dishes; and a delicious local soft drink called Sorrel, which is made by boiling flowers from the sorrel bush. Many of the ingredients were specially flown in from Grenada for the event. A traditional steel band, The Old Maestros, was arranged. Most of the band's members were from Toronto, having emigrated from the islands.

About six months after my appointment, I received a note from the Ministry of Foreign Affairs in Grenada requesting me to accept the additional position of Grenada's representative to the Inter-American Commission of Women. At about the same time, my staff approached me to request salary revisions. They had not received a salary increase for more than three years. I spoke with the permanent secretary of the Grenadian ministry, who suggested that I meet with the prime minister's delegation the next time he was in New York. I saw that he was to attend a United Nations session in about a month's time. I arranged for my schedule to intersect with his and booked into his hotel in Manhattan.

I arrived on time and met the prime minister and his delegation for drinks in a hospitality suite. The mood was jovial and relaxed. I paid my respects to Sir Eric, chatted with him for a while, circulated to say hello to friends and colleagues and, after confirming my appointment with the prime minister for nine the next morning, excused myself. As I slept, all hell broke loose in Grenada.

CHAPTER SIXTEEN

The Revolution Comes

M Y WAKE-UP CALL CAME as scheduled the next morning at seven, March 13, 1979. A half hour later, as I was getting ready for my appointment with Sir Eric, the telephone rang again. It was my sister Pommie. Her voice urgent, she asked if I had seen or heard the morning news.

"There's been a military coup in Grenada, Jenny. The government's been taken over by the opposition led by Maurice Bishop!"

I thought I was having a bad dream. Before I could respond, Pommie continued.

"Jenny, I don't know your job, but it would seem to me to be prudent if you left New York immediately and returned to Ottawa. What do you think?"

"Yes. Yes, I agree, Pommie. Thank you. I need first to touch base with the prime minister and delegation members. I'm almost dressed and ready. I'll go straight to JFK as soon as I've done that."

I hung up the telephone, shaking. I quickly finished dressing, picked up my briefcase and opened the door. As soon as I looked along the corridor toward the elevator, the gravity of the situation was clear. The whole floor was crawling with security men with walkie-talkies and headphones. They were moving around and speaking to each other in loud, serious tones. Two of them immediately asked me where I was headed. I said I was on my way to a meeting with the prime minister of Grenada and his delegation. One of the security men then offered to accompany me to Gairy's suite. He said nothing to me as we made our way up to the nineteenth floor. The short journey seemed to take forever.

There were more security personnel and some obvious FBI and CIA agents on the prime minister's floor. My escort tapped sharply on the door, which opened immediately. As soon as I entered, I could feel the tension.

"What's wrong?" I asked, pretending not to know anything. Sir Eric was seated at the end of the table, grim-faced and silent. Gloria Payne, permanent secretary to the ministry, offered me a chair. As soon as I was seated, she confirmed the news. Grenada had been taken by coup.

Gloria informed me that guns had been shipped into Grenada inside barrels of tar from Washington, DC. The government had received a tip about the arrival of the barrels, which were consigned to persons connected with the opposition party. Instructions had been left to arrest those responsible. It was this impending threat, she explained, that apparently pushed the opposition to act precipitately.

One of the first places taken by the insurgents was the Grenada Broadcasting Service, which the new government renamed Radio Free Grenada. It had then broadcast the following:

This is Maurice Bishop speaking.

At 4:15 a.m. this morning, the People's Revolutionary Army seized control of the army barracks at True Blue.

The barracks were burned to the ground. After half-an-hour struggle, the forces of Gairy's army were completely defeated, and surrendered.

Every single soldier surrendered, and not a single member of the revolutionary forces was injured.

At the same time, the radio station was captured without a shot being fired. Shortly after this, several cabinet ministers were captured in their beds by units of the revolutionary army. [. . .]

At this moment, several police stations have already put up the white flag of surrender.

Revolutionary forces have been dispatched to mop up any possible source of resistance or disloyalty in the new government.

I am now calling upon the working people, the youths, workers, farmers, fishermen, middle-class people and women to join our armed revolutionary forces at central positions in your communities and to give them any assistance which they call for.[1]

After speaking with Gloria, I crossed the room to where the prime minister was seated. He turned to me and spoke at last.

"Jennifer, I want you to meet with the Canadian prime minister on your return to Ottawa. Do what you can to gain his full support. Give him my telephone number in New York, and tell him I am requesting Canada's assistance in sending troops into Grenada to restore the rightful leader and government to their places."

"I will do what I can, Sir Eric."

The Canadian prime minister at this time was Joe Clark, leading his Conservative government. Pierre Trudeau was off the scene, although only temporarily. I knew almost with certainty that Canada would not, on principle, wish to become involved in this issue. As a middle power, Canada had always seen itself as a mediator and

---

1   Maurice Bishop, "Address to the Nation," Radio Free Grenada, March 13, 1979, in *The Grenada Revolution 2001–2019*, by Ann Elizabeth Wilder, on the website of the Government of Grenada.

steered clear of direct intervention in conflict situations. Diplomacy and peacekeeping, according to the renowned Canadian diplomat and former prime minister Lester B. Pearson, were the best roles for Canada internationally.

Back in Ottawa that evening, I went straight home. The Royal Canadian Mounted Police (RCMP) patrol that kept guard over my residence had been increased, and media people were camped outside, hungry for any statement I might be prepared to offer. They had been calling my office and residence for comments all day. I had to disappoint them. As soon as I was in the house, I telephoned the High Commission and spoke with my first secretary. He sounded shaken. I called a staff meeting for nine the next morning.

The Canadian government had increased my security detail because they feared for my personal safety. At the time, I did not really understand their concern—I considered myself to be politically neutral. I had never openly supported any of the political parties or individuals involved in them while in Grenada or abroad. Furthermore, Ottawa, Canada's capital, was a relatively safe city, and the presence of the RCMP patrol served to give me and the family a sense of security. I had yet to encounter the hostility of many members of the Grenadian diaspora, who suddenly showed their political stripes in favour of the new regime when news of the coup became known. They considered me part of the old regime.

The next morning, the *Ottawa Citizen* reported that Maurice Bishop had overthrown what he called "the government of the criminal dictator Eric M. Gairy." It added that Bishop's announcement over Radio Free Grenada had been interspersed with West Indian calypso and reggae music, and that the estimated one thousand tourists on the island, most of them North American, were believed to be in no danger.

Several days went by without a word from Grenada. During that period, we kept our office open, although it was in a state of limbo.

The phones were busy as Grenadian nationals called to enquire if there was news, but as we ourselves were in the dark, we had little to add to what had been reported. The staff felt certain that they would be recalled to Grenada or dismissed. As a result, they were distracted and were using their own resources to make contact with family and friends on the island or elsewhere. I know they all expected that I would be replaced, too, and I shared their sentiments. Concerned for their mental health and well-being, I suggested they take whatever leave was due to them. I would continue to report to work daily, hoping to receive instructions sooner rather than later.

Finally, one evening several days later, at about eleven o'clock. It was the voice of Angela Bishop, wife of Maurice Bishop. I knew Angela well. She spoke quickly.

"Jennifer. It's Angela. I'm calling from the Grenada Broadcasting Service."

"Hello, Angela. It's certainly good to hear from you. I had wondered when someone would contact me."

"Maurice has been hoping to contact you himself, but things here have been so hectic. You wouldn't believe it, but we're still holed up here at the broadcasting station. We're all sleeping here and haven't been home since this all happened days ago. Maurice has asked me to tell you that he hears you've been doing a good job up there and he wants you to continue your work until you hear from him personally."

I replied that I would continue as high commissioner for a period of six months, enough time for them to find someone of their own choosing to take over the job.

I was reminded of the Maurice Bishop I had known growing up. His father had a shop in St. George's. Maurice was a good student and involved in sports, but there was no hint of radical leanings. He had been at my wedding. Regardless, the world now knew Maurice Bishop as the revolutionary who had taken over the island in a bloodless coup while Sir Eric Gairy was away in New York.

This was no minor event. The Gairy government had taken Grenada from the status of British colony to independence in 1974, and he had been the island's first and only democratically elected head of government. Of course, he had always had opposition. Bishop had formed his party, the New Jewel Movement (NJM), in 1973 by merging two other parties. After Grenada was granted independence, Bishop's NJM became the official opposition party. As its leader, he was aligned with and under the influence of Cuba's Fidel Castro and Nicaragua's Daniel Ortega, although the extent of these ties was not yet known. Now he had succeeded in the first revolutionary overthrow of an elected government in the English-speaking Caribbean, and the first unconstitutional change of power in the Eastern Caribbean.

One of my first missions in office under the People's Revolutionary Government (PRG) was to reassure the government of Canada that it was "business as usual" in Grenada. I was summoned to the Ministry of External Affairs for a meeting with Joe Clark, who was accompanied by his minister, Flora MacDonald. I told them about my meeting in New York with Sir Eric and his request for assistance. I also told them about my call with Angela Bishop and that I knew all the players in the island's new government. Grenada is a very small place.

The meeting went well. The prime minister asked me to keep in touch and to advise them of any new developments. Soon after the meeting, Canada reported that it would recognize Bishop's PRG. It helped the PRG's cause that the Canadian High Commission in Barbados was reporting a favourable reception of the new government in the region. Canada's move was an important development amid all the uncertainty surrounding Grenada and the Caribbean.

It wasn't long before the changes wrought by the coup were felt in Ottawa. Instructions were issued for some members of staff to be changed, due to the perception of closeness with the previous government. It seemed that I was the only Grenadian head of mission to be kept on anywhere, although the governor general, Sir Paul Scoon, was still in office. I knew Sir Paul reasonably well. He had been my math tutor in high school. By keeping him on, the PRG was able to signal to the British government its desire to keep the diplomatic door open. I supposed that I had been kept for the same reason of diplomatic appearances.

Other changes included the location of the High Commission office. The PRG wanted a more central, accessible and high-profile venue in Ottawa. I obliged, although my family decided to move out of the official rented residence on Monkland Avenue and return to our family home in Osgoode. I felt that the rental was an unnecessary financial burden for Grenada, under the circumstances, and I believed I could commute daily to the office in downtown Ottawa, a distance of approximately thirty kilometres. Also, the children, who were still very young, had more space and security in a rural environment. As far as official functions were concerned, I decided to hold them at home.

One of the first events I organized back on the farm was a large autumn barbecue. It was a lot of work. Most of my colleagues left the details of entertainment to their wives. With no wife of my own, I arranged the food and drinks and other necessities myself. When my guests arrived on the appointed day, I was delighted to find among them the recently retired Pierre Trudeau. He had been invited, but his office had not been sure that he would be able to attend. As it happened, he was free, and his driver had been sent out on a dry run a day or two before learning the route.

I shook his hand and welcomed him to Osgoode and introduced him to some guests who were also happy to see him. Trudeau was always popular with the diplomatic corps. They expressed their regrets over his recent electoral defeat and wished him well. He responded that he felt like he was finally starting to live a real life outside of politics It was evident that Trudeau was in a relaxed mood. He sat talking to my mother-in-law for a long time and charmed her in his quiet, charismatic way. Before going to bed, my children, Sophia and Beau, came in their pyjamas to say goodnight, as they always did. Sophia had a Dr. Seuss book in her hand. Trudeau took her on his lap and read to her, telling her it was one of the favourites of Michel, his son. I recalled this moment years later when Michel died tragically in an alpine accident. I could imagine how hard it must have been for Trudeau; his former wife, Margaret; and their family.

A month after the barbeque, representatives of the PRG arrived in Canada to meet Canadian government officials, as well as Grenadian nationals. The delegation was led by Kenrick Radix, a lawyer and a close friend of Maurice Bishop's. I knew him too. He had been one of the group of friends with whom I had grown up, part of the wider social circle known to my brothers and me. The purpose of his visit was to reassure Grenadian nationals and the Canadian government that all was stable on the home front.

It was obvious from the speeches made by the delegation that the PRG was following a Socialist line. Its members seemed bent on criticizing the US government, which they described as imperialist. I worried that while there was a great deal of goodwill toward the new leadership, their openly anti-American sentiments were misguided.

It was clear, however, that the new regime was supported by many members of the Grenadian diaspora. Some offered to give up their jobs in Canada and return to the island to support the new regime. It was around this time that I noticed silence and unfriendliness from some Grenadian nationals who resented me for my connection to the deposed prime minister. Gairy had not been popular with progressive Grenadians. Relatively uneducated, he had authoritarian tendencies and a strong interest in Unidentified Flying Objects (UFOs). The opposition believed he was corrupt and that he did not play fair in elections, and that a coup was the only way to defeat him.

I understood my position as requiring me to represent Grenada, not a particular politician, and resolved to make the best of things. I knew Gairy's limitations. I was also skeptical of the methods the PRG had used to gain power, but we all wished the new government well and wanted to show our willingness to cooperate in the interest of Grenada.

I was amused by the reaction of some of my diplomatic colleagues to the changes in Grenada. I suddenly found myself invited to many of the embassies of Eastern Bloc and Socialist countries where I was greeted as a comrade in arms and regarded as a seasoned diplomat. His Excellency Alexander Yakovlev was the Soviet ambassador at the time and the dean of the diplomatic corps by virtue of his long tenure in Ottawa. He seemed pleased that I had been kept on by the Grenada's government: "They recognized your good work, Madam." My promotion among the left-wing countries was in strong contrast to the growing disdain I experienced as Grenada's high commissioner from the US representative. The United States was not at all pleased at the coup, the PRG's anti-American rhetoric, or its reliance on Cuba and other leftist countries for financial and moral support.

The PRG made another move that affected me directly. My first secretary, George Soltysik, was succeeded by Ian Francis, a Grenadian from Toronto. Although well connected with segments of the Grenadian diaspora, Francis lacked any diplomatic experience and found it difficult to adjust to the rules and regulations of his office. He developed a habit of claiming diplomatic immunity for his many parking and driving violations. I had to explain to him that immunity was a privilege that could not be taken for granted and that diplomats could not abuse it. I was sensitive to the fact that Canada had been gracious in bending the rules to enable me to keep my Canadian citizenship while serving as high commissioner. I had no intention of jeopardizing my position so that Francis could park where he liked, and I made that abundantly clear to my staff.

Along the way, I agreed to extend the six months that I had promised Maurice Bishop I would remain in office. As the first anniversary of the Grenadian revolution approached in March 1980, he invited me to attend celebrations to mark the occasion. It would be my first chance to see the new Grenada.

CHAPTER SEVENTEEN

The Bloody End

TRAVELLED TO GRENADA with my son, Beau. I felt I needed to spend more individual time with him. I had been very busy these past months, and he was still very young. I also knew my parents would relish the time and opportunity to get to know him better.

In my capacity as high commissioner, I invited three prominent government members to attend the anniversary celebrations: the member of Parliament Mike Forrestall and Senator Health MacQuarrie, both of whom had strong ties to the Caribbean, and Alan Rodger, Canada's high commissioner to Barbados, who had additional responsibility for the Eastern Caribbean, including Grenada. I knew these three individuals well and was convinced they were willing and able to promote Grenadian interests in Canada. They, in turn, trusted me.

From the moment I touched down at Pearls Airport, I noticed that the atmosphere in Grenada had changed. I saw several armed military personnel carrying either revolvers or rifles, which would never have happened before the revolution. I wondered what sort of reception I would receive from the new government, but those concerns were soon dispelled. Everyone appeared friendly, and made a point of calling me "Sister Jennifer." Boys and men referred to each other as "brother" in true Socialist style.

Our first meeting was held at the prime minister's residence, Mount Royal. I was shown into an informal living room to wait for my meeting to begin. The wait seemed longer than protocol required. Finally, the inner door opened, and there stood Maurice Bishop and Bernard Coard, both with huge smiles on their faces. They embraced me. They were quick to reminisce over an incident in the late 1960s at Notting Hill Gate in London when, they maintained, I saved them from certain complications with the police over an unlicensed motorcycle they were riding. I recalled playing tennis at the Tanteen courts, near my old high school, with Bernard during our school days. Such was the nature of our connections.

Our more serious business concerned Grenada's external strategy, whose focus was the first anniversary of the revolution. I briefed them on sentiments in Canada and the progress of certain development projects. The PRG had prioritized an international airport for Grenada and had approached several countries to assist with its funding. Canada and Cuba were among those asked.

The big anniversary celebration took place on March 13, 1980, at the Queen's Park in St. George's. I attended with my Canadian government guests. The speakers included Daniel Ortega, revolutionary leader of Nicaragua. Dressed in military fatigues, he spoke in Spanish, while his speech was interpreted for the benefit of the large crowd. He highlighted the solidarity of his government with that of the PRG. His was followed by Michael Manley, prime minister of Jamaica, and still later by the Cuban ambassador to Grenada.

In return, Maurice Bishop and Bernard Coard thanked by name the countries that had rendered assistance to Grenada over the past year. My Canadian guests waited to hear an acknowledgement of Canada, as did I. It was not forthcoming. We waited in vain. In spite of the fact that Canada was one of the very first countries to recognize the PRG and continued in good faith all the aid projects that had been implemented before the coup, the Canadians were shunned on this occasion. My guests were understandably upset and made this clear to me when we met later that evening for dinner at their hotel. Both Michael Forrestall and Heath MacQuarrie described the incident as "a slap in the face for Canada." I tried to downplay the unfortunate incident by suggesting it was probably a simple omission. They were far from convinced. I, too, was extremely disappointed and told them so.

The following day, Grenadian diplomats from around the world, including me, met with senior government officials as well as Bishop and Coard. The meeting focused on ways to attract more aid from foreign governments. The discussion ran on for about thirty minutes during which I remained mostly silent. Suddenly, Bernard looked at me and said, "Jennifer, what would you recommend to increase the amount of foreign aid from Canada?"

I looked him straight in the eye and replied, "Well, yesterday you had an opportunity, but you blew it."

He asked me to explain.

"Yesterday," I told him, "when you were thanking countries for their assistance to Grenada, you omitted Canada. That was the ideal opportunity for you to have thanked Canada for recognizing the government of Grenada, and it would have encouraged more aid to Grenada."

"It was not an omission," Bernard replied. "It was a deliberate tactic. By not thanking Canada, we thought they would realize they had not given enough and therefore increase future aid."

I was astounded. Shocked. Outraged. The rationale made no sense to me at all. In fact, I was so deeply ashamed that I decided there and then that my days as high commissioner for Grenada were numbered. I knew I could not work for a government with this mentality.

Some months later, I arranged, at the request of Maurice Bishop, a visit for him to Canada. I suspected that Maurice had realized his error, and the bridges he had burned, and was seeking to make amends. The urgency around arranging this visit suggested that the PRG was having second thoughts about its strategy. While still upset, I decided to use my influence in Ottawa to help overcome the negativity following the anniversary celebrations.

Maurice was accompanied on his visit by Selwyn Strachan, his mobilization minister. They made a good impression on their Canadian hosts. Maurice was eloquent and personable. One of our last meetings was with Flora MacDonald, minister of foreign affairs. She appeared to be impressed and promised increased aid to Grenada. However, within hours of leaving her office, I was told by a member of my staff that Bernard Coard, acting prime minister in Maurice's absence, had meanwhile closed the only functioning newspaper in Grenada.

This action could not have come at a worse time, and it was a surprise to Maurice. Bernard Coard seemed to have acted on his own, leaving Maurice to face the music. The Canadian media immediately latched on to the news, and I was called back to the Department of External Affairs to explain what had transpired. I was pointedly asked if I had known in advance of our meeting about the newspaper's closing. "Absolutely not," I said, which was the truth. I could tell that the minister's trust was fading.

It seemed to me that the revolution was taking a toll on Maurice. Prior to leaving Canada, he appeared preoccupied and distant. When he said goodbye to our team, there was a sadness in his eyes. From my perspective, the writing was on the wall. I was deeply disappointed in Maurice's weakness. While he had expressed surprise at the closing of the newspaper, he did not express any outrage at this most undemocratic act, nor did he rescind the action on his return to Grenada. Bernard had acted in a most untimely and thoughtless manner and seemed to have little regard for the effect his actions would have on Maurice or Grenada. He had also failed to keep his promise of holding elections within six months. Filled with foreboding about the future of the PRG, I went back to my office to draft my letter of resignation.

When news of my resignation hit the diplomatic community, I was surprised at the level of sympathy and goodwill expressed from all quarters, including the media. It did my heart good to read such commendations, but I was in no doubt about the wisdom of my decision. In subsequent months, there were reports that the United States was holding military exercises off the Puerto Rican coast. The exercises were code-named "Amber." The Grenadian government took steps to build up its military forces with the express goal of responding to the American threat.

Maurice did not last long after his return to Grenada. Disputes arose between him and other party leaders, including Bernard, over the sharing of power and what appeared to be a softening of his position on the United States. He was placed under house arrest, which sent shock waves throughout the Caribbean and, indeed, around the world. Crowds stormed the facility where Maurice was being confined and freed him. This outpouring of support for Maurice appeared to have been unexpected by Bernard and his more militant supporters, including General Hudson Austin, commander of the Grenada forces.

Bernard Coard and Hudson adhered to strict Marxist-Leninist doctrine and practice, which they wished to impose on the PRG. The military, following orders, tracked down Maurice and his supporters and, in cold blood, shot him, his pregnant mistress Jacqueline Creft, and several cabinet ministers. The naked aggression and violence, never before experienced on this peaceful island, stunned the population of Grenada as well as neighbouring countries.

Grenadians took to hiding. They were afraid for their lives and their children. Those who could get off the island did. The leaders of

Barbados and other Eastern Caribbean nations turned to the United States government for help in resolving the situation. They were concerned that what had taken place in Grenada could spread to their own unprotected countries. On October 25, 1983, President Ronald Reagan, in collaboration with several Caribbean nations, ordered hundreds of troops into Grenada. The United States justified the invasion, later termed an "intervention," as a rescue of US citizens attending the American-owned St. George's School of Medicine. Most Grenadians, in fact, viewed the invasion as something of a rescue mission. I agreed, although I would have preferred the United Kingdom to intervene instead.

An interim government was put in place to run the Grenada and was tasked with restoring democracy. Some years later, Sir Eric Gairy was allowed to return from the United States, where he had taken refuge following the coup. He continued as head of the Grenada United Labour Party (GULP) but was never again more than a spectator in government due to ill health and a reputation damaged by the revolution.

Just prior to the invasion, my sister Pommie and her second husband, Bruce, arranged for a light aircraft to fly from Trinidad to evacuate our aging parents. They were given strict instructions to pack only the bare essentials and drive to the airport that evening without telling anyone where they were going. My parents had no idea what might be waiting for them at the airport. They had been told only that Pommie had made arrangements. They arrived just as the airport was closing and looked around anxiously. A voice called out to them, "Mr. and Mrs. Hosten? I've come to take you back to Trinidad. Your family are anxious for your safety. My name is Junior, and I'm your pilot. Please follow me as quickly as possible. We must leave immediately."

Without asking questions, my parents followed Junior out of the terminal and onto the tarmac to an awaiting aircraft. Junior opened the rear door and helped them in with their two small overnight bags, shutting the door firmly behind them. Climbing into the left-hand seat in front of them, he started the two engines and proceeded to taxi toward the runway.

"Please ensure your seatbelts are securely fastened. We will be taking off in a couple of minutes, and as you will have noticed, all the taxi and runway lights have already been extinguished. We are the last flight to leave Grenada. Don't worry about the takeoff. Everything will be fine!"

Junior lined up the aircraft on the runway in darkness, eased the throttles forward and released the brakes as the aircraft started rolling. My parents gripped their seats as it increased speed. They both sighed with relief as the wheels left the ground and the aircraft climbed into the night.

At the time of the invasion, I had already returned to work with Air Canada and enrolled in university. The Air Canada staff proved most supportive, and several of my friends pooled their cargo passes to enable me to ship powdered milk, sugar and other essentials to Grenada. Jeannie Peppy, of Air Canada's staff relations department, flew with me down to Barbados, where we arranged to accompany the items to Grenada aboard a US chopper. When we landed, the airport in Grenada was teaming with soldiers dressed in battle fatigues. They were all courteous and assured me that the shipment would be distributed to the needy as promised.

My parents, in the meantime, had returned to Grenada, concerned for the security of their property. Jeannie and I set out to find them, hoping they would be at their house in the suburb of St. Paul's. When we arrived, there was little sign of movement in the area. With butterflies in my stomach, I walked to their front door and found it tightly closed and shuttered, as if abandoned. I knocked loudly and waited. There was a faint sound of movement within, but no one came to the door. I knocked again, sharply, three times.

My father called out, "Who's there?"

"It's Jenny!"

I could hear him exclaim to my mother, "It's Jenny at the door! She's here!"

The shutters were unbolted, and my parents shuffled out onto the front porch in their dressing gowns. Tears flowed as we greeted one another. I was profoundly relieved to see them standing there, looking happy and well.

The trial of those implicated in the killing of Maurice Bishop and members of his cabinet was a drawn-out affair. In the end, Bernard Coard, General Hudson Austin and those who had taken part in the massacre were sentenced to death (later commuted to life imprisonment).

Several years later, while spending the Christmas vacation in Grenada, I was invited by my friend, Archdeacon Clement Francis, to join him as he said mass at Richmond Hill prison. I said that I would be happy to go.

Once we passed through prison security, I followed Archdeacon Francis into a large room set up for the service. Among the twenty-five or so inmates were members of the infamous PRG. Bernard, his wife, Phyllis, who had been a main player; Hudson; and many others stood among the prisoners. The service began, and I was called upon to give a reading. As my name was announced, I could see surprise on the faces of the prisoners. They had not recognized me at first. Following the service, they crowded around and shook my hand. They said that they had read and enjoyed my recently published book on free trade.

Bernard told me that he had learned a great deal since serving his prison term. I was not sure whether he meant that he had taken advantage of the opportunity to study, as many do when incarcerated for a long period, or that he regretted the actions that had brought him to prison. Either way, the experience touched me. I felt sad to see these people who had once displayed such promise ending their days in this fashion.

As a child growing up in Grenada, I would never have thought its people could resort to the kind of violence that occurred following the revolution of the 1980s. The experience scarred Grenadians and to this day many are unsure of the effects of the revolution and, leaving aside the violence, whether it had a positive or negative effect overall. Some argue that it was liberating to some Grenadians, allowing them to get ahead. Others remember the revolution for undermining some of the most essential values of Grenadian society. Historians are still trying to make sense of it, trying to realize the true impact of the event.

CHAPTER EIGHTEEN

A Whole New Me

O N GIVING UP MY OFFICE as high commissioner in Ottawa, I raised my family, worked part-time at Air Canada and completed an undergraduate degree in political science from Ottawa University, then a master's degree in political science (international relations) from Carleton University in 1992. My master's thesis, on the effect of the North American Free Trade Agreement (NAFTA), between Canada, the United States and Mexico, on Commonwealth countries in the Caribbean, was published in book form, which is how my friends in Grenada found it. My goal in all this effort was a worthwhile and stable career with the government of Canada, and particularly its international development agency (CIDA).

Before I could apply for work in international development, I was persuaded by another branch of the Canadian government to manage an anti-racism campaign, which I did for three years in the early 1990s. I then turned my attention to the field in which I was trained, joining CIDA and working on environmental projects in several developing countries, including Eritrea, Ethiopia, India and Thailand. While there, I was approached by Caricom (short for Caribbean Community) consultants who were formulating options for dealing with NAFTA's impact on the islands. There was anxiety among English-speaking Caribbean nations that they would be left out in the cold as North America consolidated its trade. My thesis had argued that the appropriate response for the Caribbean region was to integrate its own trade. Otherwise, it would always be waiting for handouts from so-called developed countries. The issue was right up my alley.

The Caricom consultants offered me a short-term contract based in St. Lucia, and it came at a good time. My husband, David, had just been declared redundant at the company where he had worked for twenty years. He was feeling rather sorry for himself and encouraged me to accept the assignment saying, "We need the money." The plan was for us to relocate to St. Lucia, headquarters of the Organization of Eastern Caribbean States (OECS), for at least a year.

The offer was a good one. I would be a technical adviser on trade to the OECS, and CIDA agreed to my taking a leave of absence for a year. I accepted. In spite of his encouraging me to take the assignment, David told me just a few weeks before I was due to leave that he would not be joining me. He was going to start a small company in the computer service field and could not get away. We would instead work out a schedule of rotating visits. This did not sit well with me, but I was not in a position to change direction after all the arrangements had been made and confirmed.

With the help of friends in St. Lucia, I found an apartment in the Cap area, which I fitted out with everything I needed to function as a consultant: laptop computer, printer, telephone, fax machine and lots of shelving for documents and books. I also had a desk at the OECS, where I worked alongside junior and senior officers. It wasn't long before I was confronted with the realities of working on the islands: I may have had a desk, but it would take a month for my computer to arrive. The Caribbean pace of work is laid back. It also took me a while to develop trust and camaraderie with my colleagues. I may have seen myself as an islander, but they saw me as an outsider—and I had to prove myself to them. Eventually, however, we did get along wonderfully, and I was impressed by their skill and dedication to the cause of Caribbean unity.

The OECS was only several years old when I arrived in St. Lucia. Comprising the smaller English-speaking countries of the Caribbean, it was once thought to have the best chance of forming a regional political unit, but that hope more or less evaporated after a number of wasted opportunities. My assignment was to help the OECS chart its own course through the fast-changing world of international trade as new trade agreements in Europe and North and Latin America came on stream and the World Trade Organization continued to evolve. I was the lead consultant on these strategic considerations, and I also worked with Caricom's team of negotiators, who attended various free-trade negotiations throughout the Americas.

Not much would be accomplished during my year in St. Lucia, largely because of the presence of a small group I often referred to as the Caribbean Elite. Sir Shridath Ramphal of Guyana and Sir Alister McIntyre, who was born in Grenada, had long histories in Caribbean affairs and controlled the so-called Regional Negotiating Machinery (RNM). They had their own ideas about how to develop the Caribbean economy, and although their ideas had been tested and found wanting in previous decades, they stood in the way of other ideas, and nothing got done. Ramphal and McIntyre horded information and failed to lead or communicate with the rest of us. We all felt alienated from the process. When our team of consultants finalized its study, we got no substantive feedback and no direction on next steps.

The Caribbean Elite was its own little club, pursuing its own narrow objectives, regardless of whether or not they were in the best interests of the Caribbean people. For example, the Regional Negotiating Machinery (RNM), an offshoot of Caricom, was originally headquartered at the Caricom base in Georgetown, Guyana. When Ramphal and McIntyre got involved, their first priority was to argue that Caricom was not competent to run RNM (or, to put it another way, that they, as leaders of RNM, should not be answerable to Caricom). They masterminded a move to separate the headquarters of RNM from Caricom, moving it to Barbados and London, conveniently at Ramphal's home office.

I attended the 1998 meeting at which the move was decided. It was a hugely important gathering involving the heads of government of at least seven countries. I was shocked by what I saw. In the middle of the meeting, there was a sudden roar of voices, and many of the men in the room were throwing their arms in the air. I asked the person next to me what the furor was about. I was told they were all listening to a cricket test match between India and the West Indies over portable radios, using earpieces. The West Indies had just taken a wicket. The meeting immediately adjourned for a half hour amid loud laughter and banter about who had scored and how. To my surprise—I suppose I had been in Canada too long—this disruption of a serious meeting in the name of cricket was quite acceptable to most in the room.

Another surprise I encountered working in St. Lucia was the way women were addressed by men. Invariably, regardless of their age or status, we were called "darling" or "sweetheart." On many occasions, I was tempted to challenge these patronizing terms. Instead, I bit my tongue, understanding that I alone could not buck a patriarchal system so deeply entrenched, especially if I wanted to be effective in my position. I was forced, it felt, to accept the status quo.

I felt wiser by the end of my year in St. Lucia. My eyes had been opened to the very real challenges facing the regional integration movement. I left believing that nothing would change in the region without an abandonment of self-interested leadership and an opening of the political system to new faces and new ideas. My own work, and that of my colleagues, had shown that the economic prospects for an insular, atomized Caribbean were severely limited. It needed to integrate and gain strength through numbers. No person is an island, even in the islands.

To this day, the Caribbean lives in a bubble, and one of these days, I fear, it will burst. Governments in the region need to prioritize and significantly improve education and health care services and offer tax incentives to encourage nationals to return home. I am not confident that existing leaders have the courage or determination to do what is necessary. Meanwhile, the Caribbean's people, its most valuable resource, leave in hordes in search of opportunities and a higher standard of living in other parts of the world. Unless this trend is reversed, the islands will always be in the periphery of true development.

Unhappily for my family and me, my marriage to David Craig was on the rocks by year's end. In hindsight, I should have seen this coming. Our children had grown up. Sophia was teaching environmental studies in Grenada, and Beau was teaching snowboarding at Whistler in British Columbia. David was at loose ends in his career and suffering something of a mid-life crisis. We had enjoyed a fairly good marriage for twenty-eight years, but now the nest was empty and it was clear, after lengthy counselling sessions and my best efforts to save the marriage, that it was over. I was thankful that both children, now fine, independent adults, were mature and fair-minded enough to take a supportive stand.

Returning to CIDA and the Ottawa area, I now needed somewhere to live. The house I chose belonged to Guyanese friends. I had visited it in the past and expressed my admiration for its warmth and character. They called me one day out of the blue, saying that they were moving back to Guyana and asked if I was interested in their property. It was located in a small village thirty minutes south of Ottawa and had 240 feet of frontage on the Rideau River, with a boathouse with an apartment above. It brought me cheer in the sad circumstances of my broken marriage. I decided to make it into a duplex, which would make the property more affordable for me. I obtained a mortgage from my bank and started renovating.

CHAPTER NINETEEN

Fighting for Justice

ON RETURNING TO CANADA, I resumed my career at CIDA and worked happily there in a variety of capacities through the 1990s and into the new millennium. The assignments I received took me all over the globe, and each was rewarding in its own way. It would take another book to do justice to my experiences in each of the countries I visited, so I will simply relate here a couple of stories about the ongoing struggle for democratic rights and women's rights that I witnessed in different parts of the world. Both issues are deeply important to me.

I started as a country analyst in the Central and Eastern European Branch of CIDA with a focus on the Ukraine, as it was struggling to make the transition from Soviet domination to independence with an open democratic government and a market economy. I later moved from there to the South East Asia division. That landed me in Pakistan in early 2001.

Approximately two years before my arrival, Nawaz Sharif's democratically elected government had been overthrown in a military coup led by the head of the Pakistan army, General Pervez Musharraf. A brilliant politician, Musharraf argued that the coup was necessary to save Pakistan from massive corruption and economic incompetence.

He made some smart moves, such as devolving or decentralizing government services to the local level in order to improve services, which all Pakistanis agreed were wanting. He also moved to allow more participation by civil society in government and to encourage women in politics. He promised to restore democracy, starting at the local level.

It was not the easiest thing to believe a military dictator's promise to improve governance, but Canada took Musharraf at his word and continued to provide aid to the country's economically deprived masses. He came through, and there was great excitement on the ground when local elections were announced, with support from Canada, the European Union and the United States.

My role included managing a program to support Pakistan's efforts to strengthen public participation in governance and the inclusion of women in local politics. CIDA was a great supporter of a non-governmental organization called Aurat (which means "woman" in Urdu), founded and led by the dynamic Nigar Ahmad. She was a tireless campaigner for women in governance and reproductive rights, and against domestic violence. Her organization had a strong grass-roots network across the country, and it was effective in the elections.

The results of the voting were impressive. Many local government seats had been won by women (although in some cases, men had put their wives or sisters forward and were pulling the strings). As one might expect with a first-time experiment in democracy under the auspices of a dictator, the population was split in its support of the election results. Some saw the hand of General Musharraf in the outcome, while others believed the vote was entirely legitimate. Supporters of the process were especially pleased that the elections had uprooted Islamic groups from some of their strongholds in the North-West Frontier province.

I attended one of the first meetings of an elected local council, along with some of my colleagues a few weeks after the elections. The newly elected members representing a particular village were evenly split between men and women. After formally opening the meeting, the chairman promptly addressed the women councillors in Urdu. I requested a translation from one of my Pakistani colleagues.

"He asked the women councillors to turn around and face the wall."

"Why has he asked them to do this?"

"Well, he does not think that women should look at or address the men."

I was aghast and sat wondering how I would report this turn of events back to Canada.

One of my colleagues protested the chairman's request: "Excuse me, sir. These women were duly elected as councillors, and you have asked them to face the wall, meaning that they will not be able to do what they were elected to do. They have more rights than you, considering they were elected and you were not."

There was a tense discussion in the room lasting ten minutes or so. The chairman then announced in Urdu that the women councillors could turn and face the front of the room. The audience clapped, and the chairman lowered his eyes in embarrassment. The meeting continued, although it ended earlier than expected with no substantive decisions taken.

It seemed strange to me that Pakistan, which had elected one of the first women prime ministers in history, Benazir Bhutto in 1988, would still be struggling to accept the political equality of women. I was told that Pakistanis regard Bhutto, the daughter of a former prime minister, a person of great wealth and a member of the nation's elite, as an anomaly. It did not help that there was corruption in both of her administrations. In any event, it was clear to me that whatever progress had been made in these recent elections, there were miles to go before women would be accepted as equal participants in Pakistani democracy.

One morning, six months after I joined CIDA's Pakistan program, I was to host a small meeting of Canadian and Pakistani officials in Ottawa. As I drove to the venue in the west end of the city, I listened in horror and disbelief to a news flash on the radio recording the crash of first one, and then another, Boeing 767 commercial jetliner into the towers of the World Trade Center in New York City. These tragic events sent shock waves around the world. They heralded a new era of terrorism by Islamic extremists and led to wars in Afghanistan and Iraq.

Much less consequentially, 9/11 had a negative effect on CIDA's work in Pakistan and spelled an end to my assignment in that country. After the explosion of a bomb in a Christian church in Islamabad, resulting in the injury of one of my colleagues, Pakistan was declared an unsafe post. I was among the last CIDA workers to leave Peshawar. Despite all of this, I made wonderful friends in Pakistan and enjoyed my time there immensely. Years later, when my daughter Sophia and her husband, Brett, announced their intentions to accept contract work in Islamabad, I gave them my blessings and hoped they would derive as much pleasure from Pakistan and its people as I had been fortunate enough to do.

In 2002, I accepted a two-year posting with CIDA as a Canadian diplomat and aid worker in Bangladesh. I took the long route to my new post, through Bali, where I spent several weeks relaxing and reading. Whenever I met people, I identified as Canadian. I was Grenadian born, but I had now spent a greater part of my life in Canada. I was pleased to note that perceptions of Canadians were always positive, even if some people in Bali could not understand why I would leave a tropical climate for a northern one.

My arrival in Bangladesh at ten at night on August 30, at the end of monsoon season, is something I'll never forget. I was met by John Moore, head of aid with the Canadian mission. He greeted me and made arrangements for my luggage to be processed and taken to a waiting embassy car. I turned around and noticed swarms of people hanging off the fence that surrounded the airport. I was not sure if they were waiting for loved ones to arrive or, more likely, just watching to see what was going on at the airport. Either way, it hit home to me that Bangladesh, with 1,165 people per square kilometre, has by far the densest population of any large country on the planet.

Staff at the Canadian High Commission lived comfortably in the Gulshan area. The guest houses were newly renovated. We had access to cooks and drivers, as well as the Canadian Club, with its restaurant, tennis and swimming pool, located in Dhaka, the capital. It was impossible not to notice and be discomfited by the contrast between a diplomatic standard of living and that of most people in the host country. Bangladesh remains one of the poorest countries in the world, dependent largely on a garment industry and tea exports. Its average daily wage in 2002 was $1.50. There was some consolation in the fact that we were there to help the Bangladeshis, not to exploit them.

Most of the programs in my portfolio were concerned, to some extent, with promoting the welfare of women in this Muslim-majority country. The tools were legal aid, education, employment opportunities and a program aimed at women who had been disfigured in acid attacks, usually acts of vengeance by partners. It was worthwhile work, but one wondered how much real or long-term benefit was delivered.

Rokaya, an attractive and intelligent woman in her twenties, provides an example of the ongoing challenge to working women in Bangladesh. She was employed by a Canadian agency with which we worked in support of the Rural Maintenance Programme (RMP). The program's objective was to recruit forty thousand destitute women and put them to work maintaining rural roads, which were often flooded and washed away during the wet months. The RMP women worked long, hard days, carrying heavy woven baskets of dirt on their heads to fill potholes on the roads. They were paid the equivalent of $1.50 per day, out of which a quarter was banked as savings. Each woman had a bank book and learned about basic banking procedures. The duration of the employment was four years, and in the final stages of their terms, they were taught the basics of micro-enterprise. Eventually, some of these once-destitute women were able to join the community with respect and dignity as small business owners. It was a program that gave me satisfaction and joy.

One day, Rokaya paid a visit to the local town hall to look after some business. Like some of the RMP supervisors, she was given the use of a small motorcycle to enable her to get around in the course of her work. With only a quick meeting to attend, she stopped her motorcycle outside the building, behind a four-wheel-drive Toyota. From inside the building, Rokaya heard the sound of an impatient car horn and immediately excused herself from the meeting to move her motorcycle.

As she approached, the Toyota's owner unleashed vicious threats and abuse at her. No sooner had she mounted her bike than the man put the Toyota in gear and pushed her over, along with her bike, in the street. He then got out and kicked her as she lay in the dirt. As is typical in Bangladesh, a crowd gathered to offer opinions on the situation. There was a lot of waving and high-pitched shouting. Rokaya, covered with cuts and bruises, was advised by the crowd to follow her assailant into the building, which he had now entered, to offer her apologies for upsetting him. Rokaya refused the advice on principle, adding that she intended to charge him with assault.

Rokaya was accompanied by one of her colleagues to the hospital, where her bruises and abrasions were carefully documented and treated. A full report was handed over to the local police. Some weeks later, when the case was called, the magistrates dismissed the charges. It appeared that the records had been tampered with at the police station. The medical report stated that Rokaya had suffered from "low blood sugar" rather than wounds from her assault. Fortunately, a copy of the original documents had been kept, and with the help of the Bangladesh Legal Aid Society Trust (BLAST), an appeal was launched.

As the RMP project officer, and because I was interested in the case, I accompanied Rokaya to the Bogra district courthouse. The building was old, dirty and run down. It recalled a bygone era, as did the justice practised within. Accused prisoners awaiting trial were crouched and chained like animals at the back of the court, while lawyers sat in a row on backless wooden benches at the front. As we awaited Rokaya's case to be called, it became obvious to us that influence was being exerted by the well-connected defendant, who fraternized openly with police officers in the court, slapping their backs, sitting and joking with them. When our case was finally called, the judge looked down at the documents before him and, without looking up, declared the case postponed for three months.

"But Your Honour, on what grounds?" protested the BLAST lawyer.

"I am not required to provide you with a reason."

We were all shocked and more determined than ever to seek justice. The BLAST lawyer advised us that the only way we might succeed was to have the case removed from Bogra. The papers were duly filed to transfer the case to Dhaka. It took a long time to implement, like everything else in the Bangladesh legal system. In the meantime, I was advised that Rokaya and her family were receiving threats to their lives. She was issued a mobile telephone and reassigned from the field to indoor work.

When the case was finally called in Dhaka, we were advised by BLAST that it no longer felt it was the best advocate for Rokaya. Another lawyer was sought. On the day of the hearing, the new lawyer called in sick. Frustrated, I spoke with John Moore, Canada's head of aid, requesting permission to obtain the services of Sigma

Huda, the Canadian high commissioner's lawyer in Bangladesh. I had come to know Sigma through a mutual friend and had invited her and her sister, Kushi, to our residence for dinner. By no strange coincidence, Sigma's husband was the minister of communications in the Bangladeshi government.

From the time Sigma took on the case, events turned around in Rokaya's favour. For instance, on the day of the hearing in Dhaka, confirming the transfer of the case from Bogra, we learned that the entire legal file on Rokaya had gone missing. Our new legal team demanded that the court produce the documents or be charged with negligence. The documents immediately turned up, the transfer of the case went ahead and a date set for two months hence. When the appeal was finally before a newly appointed female judge, the defendant (who was not present in court) was found guilty and an arrest warrant was issued. He appeared to have fled the country. Approximately six months later, on his return to Dhaka, he was arrested and jailed.

The Rokaya case has become a landmark in Bangladesh. Women in that country are now cautiously optimistic that the page is turning and that it is finally possible to obtain justice in a thoroughly patriarchal society. Of course, there is still a long way to go.

My experience in Bangladesh underscored for me the challenges of development work. Things are not always what they seem. Politics in Bangladesh were for many years led by two women. One as head of the country, the other as head of the official opposition party. Yet the challenge of women's rights remains one of the country's biggest obstacles. While some progress can be seen in the field of education and employment mobility, it has become clear that real change depends on a combination of factors: social, structural, cultural and attitudinal in addition to political.

Bangladesh also left me with a bad back, which I attributed to long days of travel on its rough rural roads (also, a minor car accident in Ottawa did not help). In 2004, not wanting to return to a desk job in Canada, I took early retirement from the Canadian government and returned to Grenada for another adventure, this one as a businesswoman on one of the world's great beaches.

CHAPTER TWENTY

Hurricanes and Living History

O N SEPTEMBER 7, 2005, two months after I had returned to Grenada and settled into my bungalow at the north end of Grand Anse, the best beach on the island, I received an email from an old friend in Barbados, Wayne Webster, warning that a hurricane was headed my way. Generally speaking, Grenada is off the hurricane path. The only one I could remember, Hurricane Janet, occurred in 1955 when I was a child. It was rare, but it had a devastating effect that was felt for years.

I turned on the radio and heard that Hurricane Ivan was predicted to hit nearby Barbados sometime that afternoon. I decided to prepare for any eventuality. I went shopping and found candles, flashlights, but only a limited supply of batteries. As the day progressed, the wind picked up and so did the sea. By dusk the wind was howling.

I received a call from two of my nieces, inviting me to stay with them. They were concerned that I was too close to the beach. They both lived in solid, hillside buildings, which offered more protection and better drainage. Grateful as I was for their kind offers, I was concerned that leaving my place would leave me open to theft and other problems, so I declined.

At about ten that night, Grenada was hit by Ivan, a category-three hurricane. The winds, at 160 kilometres per hour (100 miles per hour) were shrieking. I did not feel safe in my house. I filled a large garbage bag with my valuables and important documents, picked up my small, frightened shih tzu dog, Kuta, and ran out to my car, partially protected by a carport. There, Kuta and I waited out the worst. She was so scared by the wind and driving rain that there was no hope of sleep (she would be traumatized by every subsequent storm). It was one of the longest nights I remember. I prayed for the Lord's protection and guidance in the moment, and in the future, because it was clear I would need all the help I could get when Ivan passed. By morning, my newly purchased bungalow was practically demolished.

Pommie, still in Trinidad and reliable as ever, came to my rescue. Within hours, my sister had emergency supplies, including tarpaulins, on their way to me by boat. I was to pick them up at the dock at six the next morning. While I had lost a roof and would have to vacate my derelict property, it was evident once I arrived at the dock that others were in far worse shape.

Recalling that the United Nations had a division of its Global Development Network in Barbados, I placed a call to see what aid could be arranged for Grenada. I was put through to the managing director, whom I had known from my CIDA days in Ottawa. Rosina Wiltshire was happy to know that I was in Grenada and immediately asked me to accept a temporary assignment to assist with an aid effort for Grenada. Without too much thought about what would be involved, I agreed to do all I could. I was almost immediately serving as the contact between the United Nations and the Grenadian government.

Power was out all over the island, buildings were damaged and most government offices were unable to function normally. The prime minister's office was operating out of the prime minister's home. Fortunately, the National Disaster Management Agency (NADMA), responsible for coordinating emergency services and supplies in times of crisis, was situated in one of the oldest and best-preserved forts on the island, Fort Frederick, built by the French in 1779 at the top of Richmond Hill. The agency had been spared the worst and was functioning well.

For the next three months, I was absorbed with coordinating relief efforts, which included Grenadian agencies, the United Nations, as well as Britain and the United States, and fighting to avoid overlap and achieve maximum effectiveness. This meant a lot of meetings, note taking and reporting back to the UN. Our priority was to keep lines of communication open and aid moving, despite so much of the island's infrastructure having been damaged or destroyed.

I enjoyed the work and felt useful in the early days of the relief; but it eventually became clear to me that I was having my own delayed response to living through Hurricane Ivan, and it was starting to take its toll. My weak spot, since my Bangladesh days, was my back. I found it increasingly difficult to sit through long meetings and stay at my computer hour after hour. After several months, on the advice of my doctor, I resigned my temporary position with the UN. I had done what I could, and by then, others had joined the team from overseas and were able to take our efforts to another level. I now had to attend to my own rebuilding needs.

Erik Johnson, a friend and local architect, came to my rescue. He prepared a damage estimate for my insurance company. The insurance money would enable me to plan a new building. I decided on a structure suitable for a bed and breakfast. In the weeks ahead, I lived in rental facilities nearby and helped supervise the construction of what would later be Jenny's Place.

Jenny's Place opened in August 2005, and I ran it as a bed and breakfast, with bar and restaurant, for a decade. Operating a small business in Grenada, with its layers and layers of red tape, was a challenge, but we developed a good reputation and became a popular destination for visitors from all parts of the world.

When I sold Jenny's early in 2018, I received many letters from people who had stayed with us over the years. They were disappointed that one of the last few locally owned properties on the island had been sold. It was time for me to move on, however, and spend more time with my family.

I had tried marriage twice more after David Craig. Both efforts were unsuccessful, despite my best efforts. My second husband was British and Australian. He joined me in Bangladesh and for a while in Grenada but due to numerous challenges, we divorced and he returned to Australia. My third attempt was made with optimism but rather impulsively before I was to have knee surgery. Before long, we found we were severely incompatible and parted. Both marriages were for the wrong reasons, one on the rebound, the other for practical reasons rather than love. They taught me a great deal about myself and what it takes to have a successful marriage.

Because my children were in Canada with families of their own, I headed north and reinvented myself once more. In 2009, at the age of sixty, I began a degree in psychology and trained to be a psychotherapist. Before completing my thesis, I secured a practicum position with Native Child and Family Services of Toronto. I had always been interested in Canada's First Nations, and this position enabled me to get a much better understanding of the culture and challenges they face. After completing my degree requirements, I obtained my first counselling position with Addiction Services for York Region. It surprised me that the issues of addiction were so widespread in what was generally considered an up-and-coming part of the greater Toronto area.

Despite coming to this field later in life, I have enjoyed my work as a psychotherapist and counsellor. I do believe it is never too late to do something that really interests you. So much the better if it allows you to assist others. The opportunity to listen and develop what is called a therapeutic relationship, based on trust and respect, is fundamental to bettering ourselves and those around us. I can honestly say that I have benefited as much from my clients as they have from me. In this way, I feel that I have been doubly blessed.

In 2010, I received a phone call from someone at BBC Radio 4, who said the network wanted to interview all of the key participants in the Miss World 1970 program, including myself, the women's liberation activists, Sally Alexander and Jo Robinson, host Michael Aspel, and Peter Jolly of Mecca. The title of the program was *The Reunion*, hosted by radio personality Sue MacGregor, and the episode would air in September 2010.

The interview was significant in several ways. It was my first opportunity to see some of these individuals after so many years. It was also the first time I met Sally Alexander and Jo Robinson and heard them speak. They still denounced pageants and stood by their protest. While I agreed with them on the need to promote women's rights, I still found them reactionary during the interview. (They chastised Peter Jolly on air for the harmless offence of saying "ladies" rather than "women," which to me is nitpicking—there are far more important issues facing women.) But despite decades of being placed in opposition to one another in the narrative that resulted from the 1970 pageant, we found we had more in common than we expected. We finally had an opportunity to connect as women. We came at things from different experiences and perspectives, but we shared deep concern for women's rights and racial equality.

"Miss World 1970" received great feedback. I was contacted by a California group seeking the rights to produce a stage play on the pageant as well as by others who saw the story as a documentary opportunity. There was also an inquiry from Left Bank Pictures in the United Kingdom. This up-and-coming film company, now best known for such well-regarded films as *The Damned United*, and the sensational Netflix series *The Crown*, wanted to secure the rights to my story as Miss World 1970.

I contacted an entertainment lawyer in Toronto and contracted to give Left Bank Pictures the rights to portray me in what would eventually become the movie *Misbehaviour*. And then, apart from a couple of contract renewals, nothing happened. Not a peep. I had just about forgotten the contract existed when eight years later, I was advised that much, in fact, had happened: a script had been approved, intensive research had been conducted, and the funding had come through. The movie was scheduled to start filming in 2018.

I was visiting my brother in France when the producers of the film requested my presence in the United Kingdom to discuss the project with its director and other key figures. In June 2018, I travelled by train from downtown Paris, Gare du Nord, to St. Pancras station in downtown London and had my first in-person meeting with the people to whom I'd signed over my story.

I was shown the draft script and asked to provide comments. I was assured that the production would portray me and others accurately. I was told that the story was being pitched as a drama-comedy and that, to my surprise, my character would be a leading one in the movie. I had originally thought it would be about the protests and that I would be a bit character.

The actress due to play my part, I was informed, was Gugu Mbatha-Raw, a British actress of mixed racial heritage like me. Her name was not familiar to me, but when shown a photo of her, I recognized her from several recent movies. One that particularly stood out was *Belle*, a true story based on the campaign to abolish slavery in Britain, in which Gugu had played the leading role of Daido. I was pleased to know she would be portraying me.

In late October, I received an email from the movie's director, Philippa Lowthorpe, asking me if she could give my email to Gugu, who wanted to contact me. I replied that I would be happy to talk with her. To my surprise, Gugu wanted to meet me and see where I had grown up in Grenada as part of her research to play my role in the movie. "I have never before played the part of someone who is actually alive," she said.

After some consideration and discussion with my daughter, Sophia, it was decided that she and I would travel together to Grenada to meet with Gugu and her delightful mother, Anne Raw, a retired British nurse. It was a memorable visit. We got to know each other over the course of a week, staying at one of the locally owned hotels on Grand Anse Beach. We swam daily, had long chats and explored the island, including the Church Street home over my father's law office where I had lived throughout my childhood.

I mentioned to Gugu when we were together that I still had the gold dress that had been stolen and eventually found on the night I won the Miss World contest. She was intrigued and asked if I would consider lending the dress to the film crew for the movie. I was happy to do so, and some weeks later, I received a request from one of the producers and the director to loan them my dress. Arrangements were made to transport it to the film studios in London. Gugu, whose size is similar to mine in 1970, tried it on, and it fit her very well. I was excited at the thought of this piece of my history being of use so many years later, but apparently, the dress did not make the movie's final cut.

I never felt Gugu watching me, scrutinizing me, during the time we were together on the island, yet I saw a preview of *Misbehaviour* in January 2019 and was spellbound. Gugu played my part to perfection, every tic and gesture, and even my accent. I am confident the movie will be a success.

It is amazing to me that fifty years later, the Miss World 1970 contest is still a piece of my life and still of interest to others. It is humbling to think that some very smart film people believed it warrants a feature movie that will bring those events to an entirely new audience today.

Beauty Contests and Other Blessings

ONE AFTERNOON IN 1989, while sitting in on a University of Ottawa course titled Women in Politics, I was reminded of the part played by beauty contests in the feminist movement. The class was reading from one of Germaine Greer's books on feminism in which she referred to the 1970 Miss World Contest as a landmark in the rise of the women's movement. I was sitting next to a fellow student, Myrna, who has since become a close friend. Something of a media buff, she knew I had once been a beauty contestant and asked me quietly what I thought of the subject. I put my index finger up to my mouth—*shhh*. "I will talk with you later," I said.

Afterward, when Myrna pressed me for my opinion, I told her,

I take a developmental approach in arguing in favour of beauty contests. They provide young women with an opportunity to improve themselves by enabling them to be the best they can be. They gain experience by appearing in public, talking to audiences and engaging with media. Other benefits can include the opportunity to travel abroad, develop knowledge of other cultures and form life-long friendships. Many participants also develop life skills such as time management and social etiquette. In short, most learn to over-come personal hurdles and use the experience as a stepping stone to other careers. Christie Brinkley went on to be a supermodel. Halle Berry, an actress. There are countless more examples, including at least three Miss Worlds who became medical doctors and one or two who became engineers. I myself became a spokeswoman for my country. So while the feminist movement speaks of using the Miss World contest to raise the profile of its cause, I like the way Cindy Breakspeare, a former Miss World from Jamaica, presents the case for pageants: "Nobody exploited me. I exploited myself. I saw this as a great opportunity to further my career, and I went for it!"

As a result of its link to beauty contests, feminism, as a cause, has become better known. However, feminists themselves don't always follow their own logic. True feminism, in my eyes, gives women the choice to pursue their desires. Simone de Beauvoir spoke admirably on the importance of choice: "How chance and choice converge to make us who we are." All women and men should be free to follow their own paths, to use what God has given them to the best of their ability. None of us are required to choose what might be considered traditional types of work or to submit to one particular movement or theory. That women have more choices and options today, I think, is largely due to the success of feminism. We need to build on choice, not backtrack.

I commend the organizers of beauty contests (some more than others) for bringing these events in line with current thinking about empowering women to make wise choices. This includes omitting or minimizing the importance of the swimsuit component, which had in the past served to objectify women. Pageants now put more emphasis on an individual's ability to communicate intelligently and represent women around the world. This is all positive. Again, there is no one roadmap for personal development, and women should not have to apologize to anyone for choosing the route of the beauty contest while on their path to finding themselves and their true calling.

It is hugely significant to me that at the time of this writing, five of the major pageant winners are black women. This tells me that a lot of young women, including many who do not come from privileged backgrounds, are finding these contests useful stepping stones to self-betterment and fulfillment. My participation in the Miss World contest in 1970 took me on an adventure that continued for the rest of my life.

My life has been truly blessed. I have lived in Canada, one of the wealthiest nations in the world, and I have worked in Bangladesh, one of the poorest. This range of experiences taught me that people are the same wherever you go and ensures that I never forget how fortunate we are in the Western world. Three-quarters of the world's population lives one day to the next, in fragile circumstances. Those of us in more prosperous countries have an obligation to help others, showing them empathy, giving real assistance when we can and not behaving in an exploitive manner. These are the values that make us true citizens of the world. That is the sum of my learnings in the field of development.

While I still value marriage, I am at a stage of life in which I enjoy being single and spending time with my family and numerous friends. I have two wonderful children and now five grandchildren. Sophia completed her master's degree some years ago in disaster and emergency management and has worked all over the world, including a difficult posting with the United Nations in Afghanistan. She now lives and works just north of Toronto in the York region. Beau owns his own property management company in Whistler, British Columbia. They both have wonderful supportive spouses.

Most importantly, they are good people who have made good choices.

It's funny, but one of the things I'm most often asked about is how I adjusted to life on a Canadian farm after all the Miss World glamour. Part of the answer is that a farm in Canada can be a great way to live, and as I've discussed, there is a lot of hard, unglamorous work involved in being Miss World. The rest of the answer is that I am an adaptable person and have always appreciated real people. I had no trouble appreciating farm life and its simple rhythms. The farming community was full of pleasant, down-to-earth people, and we accepted and respected each other as human beings.

Being brought up on a farm taught my children to appreciate nature and the value of hard work. I do not think that if I had given them the option of living in the city they would necessarily have taken it. Of course, their lives today are very different from what they knew as children. It is hard for all of us to get our heads around how relatively isolated we were back then, compared to how connected we are by technology these days.

The grandchildren, especially, like to hear stories of those "primitive" times on the farm, and I enjoy telling them. My wish for them is that they will take every advantage of the opportunities that come to them, knowing that those opportunities will take forms they could never have imagined, and take them places they could never have expected to be.